CW00889351

Central Statistical Office

"Our mission is to in̶ stimulate research and inform debate within government and the wider community by providing a quality statistical service"

Key Data

1994/95 Edition

Editor: Geoff Dennis

London: HMSO

Key Data

INTRODUCTION

Welcome to another edition of *Key Data*. This edition has undergone a complete review and following a readership survey the Editorial team have introduced a number of improvements.
New to this edition is an expanded chapter on Leisure to include topical information on Tourism and a separate chapter which brings together important facts and figures about the Economic Community.

The aim of *Key Data* is to present you with basic statistics in the main economic and social areas. The tables selected for reproduction have been taken direct from other publications, most of which are also produced by the Central Statistical Office:

Annual Abstract of Statistics
Regional Trends
Social Trends
Monthly Digest of Statistics
Economic Trends
United Kingdom Economic Accounts
United Kingdom Balance of Payments (The 'Pink Book')

The original publication is named under each reproduced table or chart, whilst within the table or chart there is normally a reference to the source of the figures.

With this variety of origins it is inevitable that the tables do not always conform to a standard presentation. Nevertheless they have in common that they relate to the United Kingdom in total unless clearly stated otherwise, that figures for less than a year are seasonally adjusted unless stated otherwise, and that where symbols are used they have the following meanings:

-	*nil*
..	*not available*
italics	*normally indicate percentages*
*	*average (or total) of five weeks*
†	*revised figure*

CSO Databank

The CSO Databank provides a wide range of data on disk, including many series from this publication. For more details about the availability of datasets, prices or to place your order please telephone, write or fax: Databank Marketing, Room 131/4, Central Statistical Office, Government Buildings, Great George Street, London SW1P 3AQ. Telephone 071-270 6081 or fax 071-270 6019. The CSO does not currently offer direct on-line access for these data but a list of host bureaux offering such a facility is available on request from the CSO.

The latest *'Government Statistics - a Brief Guide to Sources'* provides a useful list of the most important government publications containing statistics and sets out departmental responsibilities and contact points. It is available free from the CSO Library in Newport - Telephone 0633 812973.

Central Statistical Office
Great George Street
London SW1P 3AQ
August 1994

CONTENTS

Definitions and sources

Standard Regions coincide with the 11 Economic Planning Regions of the United Kingdom. They are also classified as **level 1** regions for the purposes of the European Community.

Great Britain comprises England, Wales and Scotland, excluding the Isle of Man and the Channel Islands. The United Kingdom comprises Great Britain and Northern Ireland.

For other sources see:

Guide to Official Statistics, 1990 edition (200 pages approximately, fully indexed) HMSO.

1.1 Standard regions and counties of England and Wales

Counties

Former metropolitan counties and Greater London

1 Tyne and Wear
2 Merseyside
3 Greater Manchester
4 West Yorkshire
5 South Yorkshire
6 West Midlands
7 Greater London

From: Regional Trends, 1994

Key Data 94, © Crown copyright 1994

1.2 Local authority regions of Scotland and Boards[1] of Northern Ireland

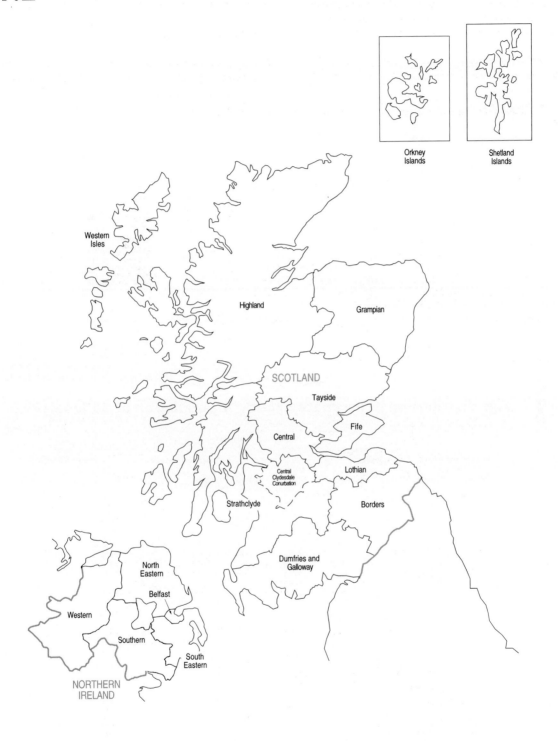

Orkney
Islands

Shetland
Islands

Western
Isles

Highland

Grampian

SCOTLAND

Tayside

Fife

Central

Lothian

Central
Clydesdale
Conurbation

Strathclyde

Borders

Dumfries and
Galloway

North
Eastern

Belfast

Western

Southern

South
Eastern

NORTHERN
IRELAND

[1] Education and Library Boards. For Health and Social Services Boards and travel-to-work areas see *Regional Trends* Appendix.

From: Regional Trends, 1994

Definitions and sources

The estimates of the resident population at mid-1991 are based on early results of the 1991 Census. They include residents temporarily outside the country and exclude foreign visitors. Members of HM and foreign Armed Forces stationed here are included, but members of HM Armed Forces stationed abroad are not.

More detailed statistics and commentaries are published in the OPCS Monitor series and quarterly publication *Population Trends*. For other sources see:
Guide to Official Statistics, 1990 edition (200 pages approximately, fully indexed) HMSO.

2.1 Mid-year estimates of resident population[1]

Thousands

	England and Wales			Scotland			Northern Ireland			United Kingdom		
	Males	Females	Persons	Males	Females	Persons	Males	Females	Persons	Males	Females	Persons
1979	24 113	25 395	49 508	2 505	2 699	5 204	755	773	1 528	27 373	28 867	56 240
1980	24 156	25 448	49 603	2 501	2 693	5 194	755	778	1 533	27 411	28 919	56 330
1981	24 160	25 474	49 634	2 495	2 685	5 180	754	783	1 538	27 409	28 943	56 352
1982	24 148	25 466	49 613	2 490	2 677	5 167	754	784	1 538	27 391	28 927	56 318
1983	24 190	25 491	49 681	2 484	2 669	5 153	756	787	1 543	27 429	28 947	56 377
1984	24 270	25 540	49 810	2 482	2 664	5 146	760	791	1 550	27 511	28 994	56 506
1985	24 369	25 621	49 990	2 479	2 658	5 137	763	795	1 558	27 611	29 074	56 685
1986	24 456	25 706	50 162	2 474	2 649	5 123	768	798	1 567	27 698	29 153	56 852
1987	24 546	25 775	50 321	2 470	2 643	5 113	773	802	1 575	27 789	29 220	57 009
1988	24 641	25 846	50 487	2 461	2 632	5 093	774	804	1 578	27 876	29 282	57 158
1989	24 750	25 928	50 678	2 463	2 634	5 097	777	806	1 583	27 989	29 368	57 358
1990	24 872	25 998	50 869	2 466	2 636	5 102	780	809	1 589	28 118	29 443	57 561
1991[2]	24 995	26 104	51 100	2 470	2 637	5 107	778	817	1 594	28 242	29 559	57 801
1992[2]	25 099	26 178	51 277	2 473	2 638	5 111	787	823	1 610	28 358	29 640	57 998

1 Figures may not add due to rounding.
2 Figures for Northern Ireland and United Kingdom are provisional.

NOTE: All the population estimates for England and Wales and for Scotland for the years 1982 - 1990 have been revised to give a smooth series consistent with both 1981 and 1991 Census results. Such revisions have not yet been made for Northern Ireland.

Sources: Office of Population Censuses and Surveys;
General Register Office (Northern Ireland);
General Register Office (Scotland)
From: Monthly Digest of Statistics, May 1994, Table 2.1

2.2 Age distribution of estimated resident population at 30 June 1992[1]

Thousands

	Resident population											
	England and Wales		Wales		Scotland		Northern Ireland[2]		United Kingdom[2]		
	Males	Females	Males	Females	Males	Females	Males	Females	Males	Females	Persons
0-4	1 771.5	1 683.1	98.3	93.6	167.3	159.1	66.4	62.9	2 005.1	1 905.1	3 910.2
5-9	1 674.0	1 584.9	97.2	92.2	164.2	156.9	67.4	63.8	1 905.5	1 805.6	3 711.1
10-14	1 607.6	1 518.9	93.8	88.6	163.6	155.9	66.0	63.7	1 837.2	1 738.5	3 575.7
15-19	1 598.6	1 508.0	91.9	86.6	165.9	157.3	65.2	60.9	1 829.6	1 726.2	3 555.8
20-24	1 984.4	1 894.5	106.0	100.4	205.5	198.4	68.7	64.1	2 258.6	2 157.1	4 415.7
25-29	2 168.8	2 086.8	107.4	1 04.8	212.0	207.6	62.9	62.9	2 443.7	2 357.2	4 800.9
30-34	1 967.8	1 913.8	100.7	100.4	199.5	197.9	57.6	59.6	2 224.9	2 171.4	4 396.3
35-39	1 711.8	1 695.6	92.2	92.8	174.2	175.5	51.7	51.7	1 937.7	1 922.8	3 860.5
40-44	1 760.5	1 756.1	99.2	98.9	169.9	172.1	48.2	48.7	1 978.6	1 976.8	3 955.4
45-49	1 700.0	1 694.9	94.8	95.2	159.5	162.1	46.3	47.6	1 905.8	1 904.7	3 810.5
50-54	1 360.9	1 362.0	79.9	79.6	136.4	143.9	38.4	39.9	1 535.7	1 545.7	3 081.4
55-59	1 281.8	1 295.2	75.2	76.8	130.0	140.7	34.9	37.4	1 446.7	1 473.4	2 920.1
60-64	1 228.1	1 305.5	73.6	78.7	123.6	140.6	31.9	37.3	1 383.6	1 483.4	2 867.0
65-69	1 129.3	1 293.2	71.5	81.5	109.7	132.9	29.4	35.8	1 268.3	1 461.8	2 730.1
70-74	919.9	1 195.2	57.6	75.3	84.5	118.0	23.3	31.5	1 027.8	1 344.8	2 372.6
75-79	638.1	987.3	38.1	59.6	56.8	94.5	15.5	24.8	710.5	1 106.5	1 817.0
80-84	389.8	761.6	22.1	45.1	33.6	70.6	8.8	17.7	432.2	849.9	1 282.0
85 and over	205.9	641.6	11.5	37.2	16.5	54.5	4.3	13.3	226.7	709.3	936.0
0-14	5 053.0	4 787.0	289.3	274.4	495.0	471.9	199.8	190.4	5 747.9	5 449.2	11 197.1
15-64	16 762.7	16 512.4	920.8	914.4	1 676.6	1 696.1	505.7	510.1	18 945.0	18 718.6	37 663.5
65 and over	3 282.9	4 878.9	200.9	298.8	301.2	470.4	81.3	123.0	3 665.4	5 472.3	9 137.7
All ages	25 098.6	26 178.2	1 411.0	1 487.6	2 472.8	2 638.4	786.8	823.4	28 358.3	29 640.1	57 998.4

1 Figures may not add due to rounding.
2 Provisional.

Sources: Office of Population Censuses and Surveys;
General Register Office (Northern Ireland);
General Register Office (Scotland)

From: Monthly Digest of Statistics, May 1994, Table 2.2

Key Data 94, © Crown copyright 1994

POPULATION AND VITAL STATISTICS

2.3 Population change[1]

United Kingdom
Thousands

		Average annual change				
	Population at start of period	Live births	Deaths	Net natural change	Other[2]	Overall annual change
Census enumerated						
1901-1911	38 237	1 091	624	467	-82	385
1911-1921	42 082	975	689	286	-92	194
1921-1931	44 027	824	555	268	-67	201
1931-1951	46 038	785	598	188	25	213
Mid-year estimates						
1951-1961	50 290	839	593	246	6	252
1961-1971	52 807	963	639	324	-12	312
1971-1981	55 928	736	666	69	-27	42
1981-1991	56 352	757	655	103	42	145
Mid-year projections[3]						
1991-2001	57 801	786	633	154	53	207
2001-2011	59 719	721	626	95	44	139
2011-2021	61 110	725	644	81	6	87
2021-2031	61 980	710	698	12	0	12

1 See Appendix, Part 1: Population and population projections.
2 Net civilian migration and other adjustments.
3 1991 - based projections based on a provisional estimate of the population of the United Kingdom of 57 649 thousand which was subsequently revised.

Sources: Office of Population Censuses and Surveys;
Government Actuary's Department; General
Register Office (Scotland); General Register Office
(Northern Ireland)
From: Social Trends 1994, Table 1.3

2.4 Age and sex structure of the population[1]

United Kingdom
Percentages and millions

	Under 16	16 - 39	40 - 64	65 - 79	80 and over	All ages (=100%) (millions)
Mid-year estimates						
1961	24.9	31.4	32.0	9.8	1.9	52.8
1971	25.5	31.3	29.9	10.9	2.3	55.9
1981	22.3	34.9	27.8	12.2	2.8	56.4
1991	20.3	35.3	28.6	12.0	3.7	57.8
Males	21.4	36.7	29.0	10.6	2.3	28.2
Females	19.3	34.0	28.2	13.3	5.2	29.6
Mid-year projections[2]						
2001	21.0	32.8	30.5	11.4	4.2	59.7
2011	19.5	30.3	33.7	11.9	4.7	61.1
2021	18.5	30.0	32.3	14.0	5.2	62.0
2031	18.4	28.7	30.3	15.6	6.9	62.1
Males	19.0	29.7	30.9	14.9	5.5	30.7
Females	17.7	27.8	29.8	16.4	8.3	31.4

1 See Appendix, Part 1: Population and population projections.
2 1991 - based projections based on a provisional estimate of the population of the United Kingdom of 57.6 million which was subsequently revised.

Sources: Office of Population Censuses and Surveys;
Government Actuary's Department; General
Register Office (Scotland); General Register Office
(Northern Ireland)

From: Social Trends 1994, Table 1.4

2.5 Conceptions: by marital status and outcome

England & Wales   Percentages and Thousands

Conceptions (percentages)	1971	1981	1990	1991
Inside marriage				
Maternities	72.6	65.9	52.3	51.9
Legal abortions[1]	5.2	5.6	4.4	4.4
Outside marriage				
Maternities inside marriage	8.1	5.5	3.9	3.7
Maternities outside marriage[2]				
-joint registration	3.5	6.8	17.6	18.9
-sole registration	4.1	4.8	6.2	6.1
Legal abortions[1]	6.7	11.4	15.5	15.0
All conceptions (=100%) (thousands)	835.5	752.3	871.5	853.7

1 Legal terminations under the *1967 Abortion Act.*
2 Births outside marriage can be registered by the mother only
  (sole registrations) or by both parents (joint registrations).

Source: Office of Population Censuses and Surveys
From: Social Trends 1994, Table 2.17

2.6 Births

United Kingdom   Annual averages or calendar years (Thousands)

	Live births				Rates				
	Total	Male	Female	Sex ratio	Crude birth rate[1]	General fertility rate[2]	TPFR[3]	Still-births[4]	Still-birth rate[4]
1900 - 02	1 095	558	537	1 037	28.6	115.1	..	..	..
1910 - 12	1 037	528	508	1 039	24.6	99.4	..	..	..
1920 - 22	1 018	522	496	1 052	23.1	93.0	..	..	..
1930 - 32	750	383	367	1 046	16.3	66.5	..	..	..
1940 - 42	723	372	351	1 062	15.0	..	1.89	26	..
1950 - 52	803	413	390	1 061	16.0	73.7	2.21	18	..
1960 - 62	946	487	459	1 063	17.9	90.3	2.80	18	..
1970 - 72	880	453	427	1 064	15 8	82.5	2.36	12	13
1980 - 82	735	377	358	1 053	13.0	62.5	1.83	5	7
1979	735	378	356	1 061	13.1	64.1	1.86	6	8
1980	754	386	368	1 050	13.4	64.9	1.89	6	7
1981	731	375	356	1 053	13.0	62.1	1.81	5	7
1982	719	369	350	1 054	12.8	60.6	1.78	5	6
1983	721	371	351	1 058	12.8	60.2	1.77	4	6
1984	730	373	356	1 049	12.9	60.3	1.77	4	6
1985	751	385	366	1 053	13.3	61.4	1.80	4	6
1986	755	387	368	1 053	13.3	61.1	1.78	4	5
1987	776	398	378	1 053	13.6	62.3	1.82	4	5
1988	788	403	384	1 049	13.8	63.2	1.84	4	5
1989	777	398	379	1 051	13.6	62.4	1.81	4	5
1990	799	409	390	1 049	13.9	64.2	1.84	4	5
1991	793	406	386	1 052	13.7	63.6	1.82	4	5
1992	781	400	380	1 052	13.5	63.4	1.80	3	4

1 Rate per 1 000 population.
2 Rate per 1 000 women aged 15 - 44.
3 Total fertility rate is the average number of children which would be born per woman if women experienced the age-specific fertility rates of the period in question throughout their child-bearing life span. UK figures for the years 1970-72 and earlier are estimates.
4 Figures given are based on stillbirths of 28 completed weeks gestation or more. On 1 October 1992 the legal definition of a stillbirth was altered to include babies born dead between 24 and 27 completed weeks gestation. Between 1 October and 31 December 1992 there were 258 babies born dead between 24 and 27 completed weeks gestation. If these babies were included in the stillbirth figures given, the stillbirth rate would be 5.

Source: Office of Population Censuses and Surveys

From: Annual Abstract of Statistics 1994, Table 2.16

Key Data 94, © Crown copyright 1994

2.7 Births and deaths

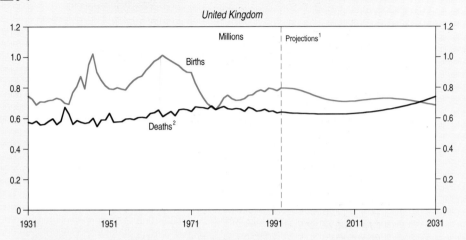

United Kingdom

1 1991-based projections.
2 Includes deaths of non-civilians and merchant seamen who died outside the country.

Sources: Office of Population Censuses and Surveys; Government Actuary's Department;
General Register Office (Scotland); General Register Office (Northern Ireland)

From: Social Trends 1994, Chart 1.1

2.8 Marriages: by type
United Kingdom

	1961	1971	1981	1991
Marriages (thousands)				
First marriage for both partners	340	369	263	222
First marriage for one partner only				
Bachelor/divorced woman	11	21	32	32
Bachelor/widow	5	4	3	2
Spinster/divorced man	12	24	36	35
Spinster/widower	8	5	3	2
Second (or subsequent) marriage for both partners				
Both divorced	5	17	44	45
Both widowed	10	10	7	4
Divorced man/widow	3	4	5	4
Divorced woman/widower	3	5	5	4
Total marriages	397	459	398	350
Remarriages[1] as a percentage of all marriages	*14*	*20*	*34*	*36*
Remarriages[1] of the divorced as a percentage of all marriages	*9*	*15*	*31*	*34*

1 Remarriage for one or both partners.

Source: Office of Population Censuses and Surveys

From: Social Trends 1994, Table 2.11

2.9 Divorce: by duration of marriage

United Kingdom			Percentages and thousands	
	Year of divorce			
	1961	1971	1981	1991

Duration of marriage
 (percentages)

	1961	1971	1981	1991
0-2 years	1.2	1.2	1.5	9.3
3-4 years	10.1	12.2	19.0	14.0
5-9 years	30.6	30.5	29.1	27.0
10-14 years	22.9	19.4	19.6	18.3
15 - 19 years	} 13.9	{ 12.6	12.8	12.8
20 - 24 years		9.5	8.6	9,5
25 - 29 years	} 21.2	{ 5.8	4.9	5.0
30 years and over		8.9	4.5	4.1
All durations (= 100%) (thousands)	27.0	79.2	155.6	171.1

Sources: Office of Population Censuses and Surveys;
General Register Office (Scotland)

From: Social Trends 1994, Table 2.13

2.10 Divorce: by sex and age

England & Wales				Rates[1]
	1961	1971	1981	1991
Males				
16 - 24	1.4	5.0	17.7	25.9
25 - 29	3.9	12.5	27.6	32.9
30 - 34	4.1	11.8	22.8	28.5
35 - 44	3.1	7.9	17.0	20.1
45 and over	1.1	3.1	4.8	5.6
All aged 16 and over	2.1	5.9	11.9	13.6
Females				
16 - 24	2.4	7.5	22.3	27.7
25 - 29	4.5	13.0	26.7	31.3
30 - 34	3.8	10.5	20.2	25.1
35 - 44	2.7	6.7	14.9	17.2
45 and over	0.9	2.8	3.9	4.5
All aged 16 and over	2.1	5.9	11.9	13.4

1 Per 1 000 married population

Source: Office of Population Censuses and Surveys

From: Social Trends 1994, Table 2.14

Key Data 94, © Crown copyright 1994

2.11 Marriage and remarriage: by sex

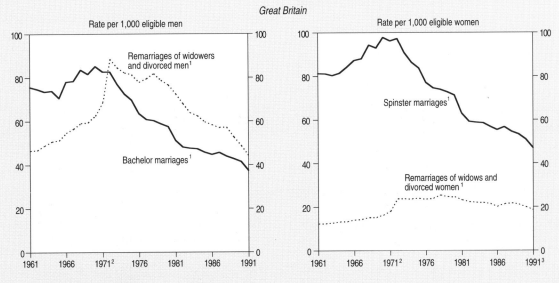

Great Britain

1 Irrespective of partners' marital status.
2 The *Divorce Reform Act 1969* came into effect in England and Wales on 1 January 1971.
3 1990 data for Scotland has been used for 1991.

Source: Office of Population Censuses and Surveys

From: Social Trends 1994, Chart 2.12

2.12 Deaths: by age and sex

United Kingdom   Rates and thousands

| | Death rates per 1 000 in each age group | | | | | | | Total |
	Under 1[1]	1-15	16-39	40-64	65-79	80 and over	All ages	deaths (thousands)
Males								
1961	26.3	0.6	1.3	11.7	65.7	193.5	12.6	322.0
1971	20.2	0.5	1.1	11.4	59.9	174.0	12.1	328.5
1981	12.7	0.4	1.0	10.1	56.1	167.5	12.0	329.1
1991	8.3	0.3	1.0	7.3	48.2	148.2	11.1	314.4
1992	7.4	0.2	1.0	7.1	47.0	148.6	10.9	308.5
Females								
1961	18.2	0.7	0.8	6.5	41.0	156.8	11.4	309.8
1971	15.5	0.4	0.6	6.3	35.3	138.0	11.0	316.5
1981	9.6	0.3	0.5	5.8	32.1	126.2	11.4	328.8
1991	6.3	0.2	0.5	4.5	29.1	112.2	11.2	331.8
1992	5.7	0.2	0.5	4.4	28.4	111.1	11.0	325.7

1 Rate per 1 000 live births.

Sources: Office of Population Censuses and Surveys; General Register Office (Scotland); General Register Office (Northern Ireland)

From: Social Trends 1994 Table 1.13

Definitions and sources

Definitional notes are given as footnotes to the tables which have been taken from the *Monthly Digest of Statistics*. The *Monthly Digest* tables refer to the United Kingdom unless otherwise stated. The charts have been taken from *Social Trends* and *Economic Trends*. More detailed statistics and commentary are published in the Employment Department's *Employment Gazette*.

For other sources see:

Guide to Official Statistics, 1990 edition (200 pages approximately, fully indexed) HMSO.

Employment Gazette HMSO.

3.1 Distribution of the workforce

Thousands

| | | | Not seasonally adjusted | | | | | Seasonally adjusted | |
| | | | Employees in employment | | Self-employed persons (with or without | | | | |
At June	Workforce[1]	Workforce in employment[1]	Males	Females	Total	employees)[2]	HM Forces[3]	Workforce[1]	Employees in employment
1989	28 671	26 928	11 992	10 668	22 661	3 497	308	28 712	22 670
1990	28 747	27 191	12 046	10 872	22 918	3 547	303	28 770	22 893
1991	28 546	26 305	11 530	10 731	22 262	3 393	297	28 554	22 220
1992	28 406	25 728	11 211	10 695	21 906	3 208	290	28 393	21 851
1993	28 176	25 311	10 929	10 622	21 551	3 178	271	28 153	21 490
1991 Q1	28 646	26 504	11 642	10 727	22 369	3 431	298	28 666	22 449
Q2	28 546	26 305	11 530	10 731	22 262	3 393	297	28 554	22 220
Q3	28 544	26 094	11 447	10 664	22 112	3 347	297	28 536	22 112
Q4	28 554	26 002	11 343	10 709	22 053	3 301	295	28 498	22 011
1992 Q1	28 521	25 813	11 228	10 675	21 902	3 254	293	28 524	21 972
Q2	28 406	25 728	11 211	10 695	21 906	3 208	290	28 393	21 851
Q3	28 208	25 360	11 042	10 508	21 550	3 211	284	28 228	21 560
Q4	28 338	25 355	10 969	10 585	21 554	3 167	280	28 296	21 523
1993 Q1	28 178	25 181	10 904	10 527	21 431	3 122	275	28 172	21 495
Q2	28 176	25 311	10 929	10 622	21 551	3 178	271	28 153	21 490
Q3	28 231	25 319	10 945	10 620	21 565	3 183	267	28 251	21 578
Q4	28 150	25 368	10 873	10 678	21 551	3 232	258	28 114	21 527

1 The workforce consists of the workforce in employment and the unemployed (claimants); the workforce in employment comprises employees in employment, the self-employed, HM Forces and participants in work-related government training programmes. For more details see the August 1988 edition of *Employment Gazette*.
2 Estimates of the self-employed are based on the 1981 census of population and the results of Labour Force Surveys. The estimates are not seasonally adjusted.
3 HM Forces figures, provided by the Ministry of Defence, represent the total number of UK service personnel, male and female, in HM Regular Forces wherever serving and including those on release leave. The numbers are not subject to seasonal adjustment.

Sources: Department of Employment; Department of Economic Development (Northern Ireland)

From: Monthly Digest of Statistics, May 1994, Table 3.1

Key Data 94, © Crown copyright 1994

3.2 Population of working age[1]: by sex and economic status[2], 1993

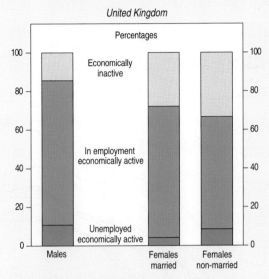

United Kingdom

1 Males aged 16-64 and females aged 16-59.
2 ILO / OECD definitions.
3 Includes those on government schemes and unpaid family workers.

Source: Employment Department

From: Social Trends 1994, Chart 4.3

3.3 Reasons for taking a part-time[1] job: by sex and marital status, Spring 1993

United Kingdom   Percentages and thousands

		Females		
	Males	Married	Non-married	All females
Student/still at school	29.4	0.6	33.4	6.9
Ill or disabled	3.3	1.0	1.3	1.1
Could not find a full-time job	29.0	8.4	18.3	10.3
Did not want a full-time job	36.2	88.0	45.4	79.9
Part-time workers[2] (=100%)(thousands)	886	4 078	967	5 045

1 Part-time is based on respondent's self assessment.

2 Includes those who did not state the reason for taking a part-time job.

Source: Employment Department
From: Social Trends 1994, Table 4.13

EMPLOYMENT

3.4 Regional unemployment rates

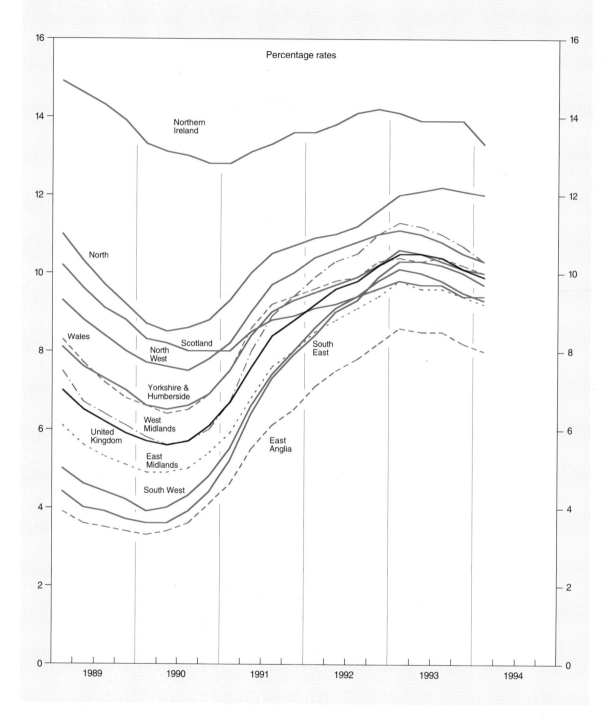

Percentage rates

Northern Ireland

North

Wales

Scotland

North West

South East

Yorkshire & Humberside

West Midlands

United Kingdom

East Anglia

East Midlands

South West

From: Economic Trends, May 1994, Chart 4.3

Key Data 94, © Crown copyright 1994

3.5 Unemployment

Thousands

	United Kingdom						Great Britain	
	Not seasonally adjusted [1,2]		Seasonally adjusted [4,5]				Seasonally adjusted [4,5]	
	Total	Percentage rate [3]	Males	Females	Total	Percentage rate [3]	Total	Percentage rate [3]
1989	1 798.7	63	1 276.1	506.0	1 782.2	6.3	1 678.8	6.1
1990	1 664.5	5.8	1 230.4	430.4	1 660.8	5.8	1 565.5	5.6
1991	2 291.9	8.1	1 734.0	552.1	2 286.1	8.1	2 187.0	7.9
1992	2 778.6	9.9	2 118.6	646.5	2 765.0	9.8	2 660.3	9.7
1993	..	10. 1	2 225.7	674.9	2 900.6	10.3	2 796.9	10.2
1991 Mar	2 142.1	7.6	1 581.1	511.0	2 092.1	7.4	1 994.9	7.2
Apr	2 198.5	7.8	1 633.9	526.0	2 159.9	7.6	2 061.9	7.5
May	2 213.8	7.8	1 688.5	543.0	2 231.5	7.9	2 133.2	7.7
Jun	2 241.0	7.9	1 743.2	556.7	2 299.9	8.1	2 201.1	8.0
Jul	2 367.5	8.4	1 796.1	571.4	2 367.5	8.4	2 267.8	8.2
Aug	2 435.1	8.6	1 833.9	581.8	2 415.7	8.5	2 315.4	8.4
Sep	2 450.7	8.7	1 863.0	588.9	2 451.9	8.7	2 351.3	8.5
Oct	2 426.0	8.6	1 891.1	595.0	2 486.1	8.8	2 384.8	8.7
Nov	2 471.8	8.7	1 922.6	599.2	2 521.8	8.9	2 420.1	8.8
Dec	2 551.7	9.0	1 946.0	601.9	2 547.9	9.0	2 446.5	8.9
1992 Jan	2 673.9	9.5	1 974.5	612.3	2 586.8	9.2	2 484.5	9.1
Feb	2 710.5	9.6	2 015.0	620.4	2 635.4	9.4	2 532.9	9.3
Mar	2 707.5	9.6	2 029.2	622.6	2 651.8	9.4	2 548.5	9.3
Apr	2 736.5	9.7	2 059.3	627.8	2 687.1	9.6	2 583.6	9.4
May	2 707.9	9.6	2 083.7	633.6	2 717.3	9.7	2 613.0	9.6
Jun	2 678.2	9.5	2 093.9	637.8	2 731.7	9.7	2 626.9	9.6
Jul	2 774.0	9.9	2 117.7	647.6	2 765.3	9.8	2 659.7	9.7
Aug	2 845.5	10.1	2 153.3	659.3	2 812.6	10.0	2 706.1	9.9
Sep	2 847.4	10.1	2 176.8	663.8	2 840.6	10.1	2 734.5	10.0
Oct	2 814.4	10.0	2 202.7	669.0	2 871.7	10.2	2 765.6	10.1
Nov	2 864.1	10.2	2 233.5	674.9	2 908.4	10.3	2 802.9	10.2
Dec	2 983.3	10.6	2 283.4	688.3	2 971.7	10.6	2 865.8	10.5
1993 Jan	3 062.1	10.9	2 275.3	687.3	2 962.6	10.5	2 857.0	10.4
Feb	3 042.6	10.8	2 271.3	687.7	2 959.0	10.5	2 853.3	10.4
Mar	2 996.7	10.6	2 252.9	680.8	2 933.7	10.4	2 828.7	10.3
Apr	3 000.5	10.6	2 257 7	684.2	2 941.9	10.4	2 837.6	10.3
May	2 916.6	10.4	2 243.3	676.4	2 919.7	10.4	2 816.3	10.3
Jun	2 865.0	10.2	2 239.9	675.2	2 915.1	10.3	2 811.5	10.2
Jul	2 929.3	10.4	2 238.2	679.0	2 917.2	10.4	2 813.2	10.3
Aug	2 960.0	10.5	2 235.3	686.2	2 921.5	10.4	2 816.7	10.3
Sep	2 912.1	10.3	2 221.5	680.5	2 902.0	10.3	2 798.1	10.2
Oct	2 793.6	9.9	2 186.6	664.3	2 850.9	10.1	2 748.5	10.0
Nov	2 769.4	9.8	2 157.3	655.6	2 812.9	10.0	2 711.5	9.9
Dec	2 782.7	9.9	2 129.5	641.3	2 770.8	9.8	2 670.7	9.7
1994 Jan	2 887.1	10.3	2 146.4	644.2	2 790.6	9.9	2 691.0	9.8
Feb	2 841.4	10.1	2 114.8	638.1	2 752.9	9.8	2 653.5	9.7
Mar	2 777.5	9.9	2 091.6	631.0	2 722.6	9.7	2 623.6	9.6

1 Unadjusted figures for 1988 were affected by the benefit regulations for those aged under 18 introduced in September 1988, most of whom are no longer eligible for income support. This reduced the UK adjusted total by about 90 000 on average, with most of this having taken effect over the two months to October 1988.

2 The unadjusted unemployment figures between September 1989 and March 1990 are affected by the change in the conditions of the Redundant Mine-workers Payment Scheme. An estimated 15 500 men left the count as a result of this change.

3 Percentage rates have been calculated by expressing the number of unemployed claimants as a percentage of the estimated total workforce (the sum of unemployed claimants, employees in employment, self-employed, H M Forces and participants on work-related government training programmes) at mid-1993 for 1993 and 1994 figures and at the corresponding mid-year estimates for earlier years.

4 The seasonally adjusted series relate only to claimants aged 18 or over in order to maintain the consistent series, available back to 1971 (1974 for the regions - see p.660 of the December 1990 *Employment Gazette* for the list of discontinuities taken into account).

5 The latest national and regional seasonally adjusted unemployment figures are provisional and can be subject to revision in the following month.

Sources: Department of Employment;
Department of Economic Development (Northern Ireland)
From: Monthly Digest, May 1994, Table 3.10

Definitions and sources

National accounts provide a comprehensive and detailed framework for describing and analysing the economy as a whole and showing how various economic activities are related. They provide the basic background for decision-taking and forecasting in both Government and business. The accounts are published annually in *United Kingdom and National Accounts: The CSO 'Blue Book'* and quarterly in *The UK Economic Accounts a quarterly supplement to Economic Trends*. A definitive detailed description of the various statistical series which comprise the national accounts is given in *United Kingdom National Accounts: Sources and Methods*. In general, the United Kingdom national accounts follow the principles recommended internationally.

Gross domestic product (GDP) is a concept of the value of goods and services produced on the economic territory irrespective of to whom the benefits accrue (United Kingdom residents or non-residents). The national product indicates the activities of UK residents only on both the UK economic territory and abroad.

The level of GDP is derived from the levels of the two broadly independent analyses of GDP based on expenditure and income. Account is taken also of the changes in volume of value added derived from the output analysis of GDP, which is compiled only in index number format.

The expenditure analysis differentiates between consumption expenditure (goods and services consumed within a short time of purchase) and investment expenditure which adds to the domestic stock of physical assets (capital formation) or to those claims on non-residents which arise from the difference between exports and imports of goods and services. Estimates are compiled in both current and constant prices. The deflator implied by these current and constant price estimates at factor cost conceptually measures the price of domestic value added and is known as the 'index of total home costs'.

The income analysis identifies the different types of factor incomes derived from domestic production such as income from employment, from self-employment, profits and rent. It is compiled only in current price terms but a constant price equivalent is derived by deflating total incomes by the total home costs deflator.

The output analysis provides estimates of the contribution of each industry. The production and construction industries account for about two-fifths of total output. Agriculture and the services industries, for example, distribution, transport, and financial services, make up the remainder. Estimates are available only at constant prices in index number form. The *Monthly Digest of Statistics* contains monthly detail for production industries.

Gross national disposable income at market prices is a concept of the United Kingdom's command over resources. It is based on GDP at market prices, adjusted for the effect of changes in the terms of trade, for net property income from abroad and net current transfers abroad.

For other sources see:

Guide to Official Statistics, 1990 edition (200 pages approximately, fully indexed) HMSO.

4.1 Gross national and domestic product[1]

£ million

| | At current prices | | | | | | At 1990 prices | | |
| | At market prices | | | less Factor cost adjust-ment[2] | At factor cost | | Gross domestic product at market prices | less Factor cost adjust-ment[5] | Gross domestic product at factor cost |
	Gross domestic product 'Money GDP'	Net property income from abroad	Gross national product		Gross domestic product[3]	Gross national product[4]			
1984	325 852	4 344	330 196	45 199	280 653	284 997	451 131	59 064	392 067
1985	357 344	2 296	359 640	49 442	307 902	310 198	468 071	60 310	407 844
1986	384 843	4 622	389 465	56 571	328 272	332 894	488 122	63 908	424 214
1987	423 381	3 757	427 138	62 706	360 675	364 432	511 615	67 798	443 817
1988	471 430	4 424	475 854	70 002	401 428	405 852	537 215	71 469	465 746
1989	515 957	3 388	519 345	74 198	441 759	445 147	548 938	72 712	476 226
1990	551 118	1 630	552 748	72 232	478 886	480 516	551 118	72 232	478 886
1991	573 645	320	573 965	78 821	494 824	495 144	538 769	71 049	467 720
1992	595 941	3 774	599 715	81 172	514 769	518 543	536 172	70 298	465 874
1993	627 985	2 703	630 688	83 755	544 230	546 933	546 742	71 821	474 921
Seasonally adjusted									
1989 Q1	125 635	1 127	126 762	18 112	107 523	108 650	136 788	18 120	118 668
Q2	127 182	834	128 016	18 530	108 652	109 486	137 225	18 327	118 898
Q3	130 075	703	130 778	18 601	111 474	112 177	137 369	18 239	119 130
Q4	133 065	724	133 789	18 955	114 110	114 834	137 556	18 026	119 530
1990 Q1	135 409	-242	135 167	19 325	116 084	115 842	138 266	18 112	120 154
Q2	136 952	-78	136 874	17 785	119 167	119 089	139 014	18 433	120 581
Q3	139 703	1132	140 835	17 721	121 982	123 114	137 543	18 029	119 514
Q4	139 054	818	139 872	17 401	121 653	122 471	136 295	17 658	118 637
1991 Q1	140 470	-448	140 022	17 811	122 659	122 211	135 184	17 707	117 477
Q2	142 969	6	142 975	20 109	122 860	122 866	134 536	17 657	116 879
Q3	144 052	407	144 459	20 395	123 657	124 064	134 391	17 715	116 676
Q4	146 154	355	146 509	20 506	125 648	126 003	134 658	17 970	116 688
1992 Q1	146 156	464	146 620	20 180	125 976	126 440	133 417	17 478	115 939
Q2	148 657	265	148 922	20 155	128 502	128 767	133 621	17 542	116 079
Q3	150 141	1480	151 621	20 214	129 927	131 407	134 393	17 608	116 785
Q4	150 987	1 565	152 552	20 623	130 364	131 929	134 741	17 670	117 071
1993 Q1	153 383	-4	153 379	20 444	132 939	132 935	135 162	17 645	117 517
Q2	155 790	315	156 105	20 896	134 894	135 209	136 186	18 085	118 101
Q3	158 100	1 263	159 363	20 970	137 130	138 393	137 198	17 994	119 204
Q4	160 712	1 129	161 841	21 445	139 267	140 396	138 196	18 097	120 099
1994 Q1	163 056	2 011	165 067	21 786	141 270	143 281	139 243	18 331	120 912

1 Estimates are given to the nearest £ million and in case of indices to one decimal place but cannot be regarded as accurate to this degree. Estimates at current market prices are affected by the abolition of domestic rates and the introduction of the community charge.

2 *Equals* taxes on expenditure *less* subsidies.

3 The factor cost estimate of GDP is obtained from the market price estimate by subtracting the factor cost adjustment..

4 Gross national product *equals* Gross domestic product *plus* Net property income from abroad.

5 *Represents* Taxes on expenditure *less* Subsidies both valued at 1990 prices.

Data in this table update those contained in CSO Blue Book table 1.1.

From: UKEA Table A1

4.2 Gross national and domestic product[1]

1990 = 100

| | Value indices at current prices | | Volume indices at 1990 prices | | | Implied gross domestic product deflator[4] | |
	Gross domestic product at market prices[2]	Gross domestic product at factor cost	Gross national disposable income at market prices[3]	Gross domestic product at market prices	Gross domestic product at factor cost	At market prices	At factor cost[5]
1984	59.1	58.6	82.8	81.9	81.9	72.2	71.6
1985	64.8	64.3	85.3	84.9	85.2	76.3	75.5
1986	69.8	68.5	88.8	88.6	88.6	78.8	77.4
1987	76.8	75.3	92.7	92.8	92.7	82.8	81.3
1988	85.5	83.8	97.7	97.5	97.3	87.8	86.2
1989	93.6	92.2	99.7	99.6	99.4	94.0	92.8
1990	100.0	100.0	100.0	100.0	100.0	100.0	100.0
1991	104.1	103.3	98.4	97.8	97.7	106.5	105.8
1992	108.1	107.5	98.3	97.3	97.3	111.1	110.5
1993	113.9	113.6	100.3	99.2	99.2	114.9	114.6
1989 Q1	91.2	89.8	99.9	99.3	99.1	91.8	90.6
Q2	92.3	90.8	99.9	99.6	99.3	92.7	91.4
Q3	94.4	93.1	99.5	99.7	99.5	94.7	93.6
Q4	96.6	95.3	99.7	99.8	99.8	96.7	95.5
1990 Q1	98.3	97.0	99.7	100.4	100.4	97.9	96.6
Q2	99.4	99.5	100.3	100.9	100.7	98.5	98.8
Q3	101.4	101.9	100.8	99.8	99.8	101.6	102.1
Q4	100.9	101.6	99.2	98.9	99.1	102.0	102.5
1991 Q1	102.0	102.5	98.7	98.1	98.1	103.9	104.4
Q2	103.8	102.6	98.7	97.6	97.6	106.3	105.1
Q3	104.6	103.3	97.8	97.5	97.5	107.2	106.0
Q4	106.1	105.0	98.6	97.7	97.5	108.5	107.7
1992 Q1	106.1	105.2	97.6	96.8	96.8	109.5	108.7
Q2	107.9	107.3	97.7	97.0	97.0	111.3	110.7
Q3	109.0	108.5	99.1	97.5	97.5	111.7	111.3
Q4	109.6	108.9	98.9	97.8	97.8	112.1	111.4
1993 Q1	111.3	111.0	98.7	98.1	98.2	113.5	113.1
Q2	113.1	112.7	99.5	98.8	98.6	114.4	114.2
Q3	114.7	114.5	100.9	99.6	99.6	115.2	115.0
Q4	116.6	116.3	102.2	100.3	100.3	116.3	116.0
1994 Q1	118.3	118.0	103.5	101.1	101.0	117.1	116.8

1 These estimates are given to one decimal place but this does not imply that
 they can be regarded as accurate to the last digit shown.
2 "Money GDP".
3 Also known as Real national disposable income (RNDI).
4 Based on sum of expenditure components of GDP at current and constant prices.
5 Also known as the Index of total home costs.

Data in this table update those contained in CSO Blue Book table 1.1.

From: UKEA Table A1

Key Data 94, © Crown copyright 1994

4.3 Gross domestic product: by category of expenditure[1]

£ million

| | | General government final consumption | | | Domestic expenditure on goods and services at market prices | | | | | | | | | | |
	Consumers' expenditure[2]	Central government	Local authorities	Total	Gross domestic fixed capital formation	Value of physical increase in stocks and work in progress[3]	Total	Exports of goods and services	Total final expenditure	less imports of goods and services	Statistical discrepancy (expenditure)	Gross domestic product at market prices	less Taxes on expenditure	Subsidies	Gross domestic product at factor cost
At current prices															
1984	198 820	44 583	26 618	71 201	55 181	1 296	326 498	91 632	418 130	92 763	485	**325 852**	52 736	7 537	**280 653**
1985	217 485	47 341	27 926	75 267	60 718	821	354 291	102 041	456 332	98 988	-	**357 344**	56 667	7 225	**307 902**
1986	241 554	50 331	30 580	80 911	65 032	682	388 179	97 885	486 064	101 221	-	**384 843**	62 872	6 301	**328 272**
1987	265 290	53 736	33 309	87 045	75 052	1 334	428 721	106 397	535 118	111 737	-	**423 381**	68 971	6 265	**360 675**
1988	299 449	57 522	36 119	93 641	91 118	4 745	488 953	107 273	596 226	124 796	-	**471 430**	76 039	6 037	**401 428**
1989	327 363	63 294	38 502	101 796	104 535	3 585	537 279	121 486	658 765	142 808	-	**515 957**	79 980	5 782	**441 759**
1990	347 527	70 108	42 826	112 934	106 776	-1 118	566 119	133 284	699 403	148 285	-	**551 118**	78 298	6 066	**478 886**
1991	365 057	77 085	47 120	124 205	96 534	-5 069	580 727	134 148	714 875	140 775	-455	**573 645**	84 816	5 995	**494 824**
1992	382 412	82 498	49 738	132 236	92 741	-1 992	605 397	140 251	745 648	149 455	-252	**595 941**	87 584	6 412	**514 769**
1993	405 871	88 112	49 954	138 066	93 147	333	637 417	157 964	795 381	166 442	-954	**627 985**	91 240	7 485	**544 230**
Unadjusted															
1989 Q1	76 092	15 616	9 352	24 968	26 852	1 050	128 962	27 701	156 663	33 164			19 015	1 651	
Q2	79 520	15 252	9 467	24 719	24 413	1 836	130 488	29 929	160 417	36 266			19 409	1 497	
Q3	84 346	15 994	9 668	25 662	26 069	969	137 046	30 659	167 705	37 438			20 657	1 365	
Q4	87 405	16 432	10 015	26 447	27 201	-270	140 783	33 197	173 980	35 940			20 899	1 269	
1990 Q1	82 112	17 171	10 147	27 318	28 269	-72	137 627	32 029	169 656	37 083			20 235	1 532	
Q2	84 381	17 189	10 534	27 723	25 248	551	137 903	33 426	171 329	38 467			18 473	1 480	
Q3	89 058	17 502	10 886	28 388	26 187	482	144 115	32 777	176 892	37 141			19 771	1 319	
Q4	91 976	18 246	11 259	29 505	27 072	-2 079	146 474	35 052	181 526	35 594			19 819	1 735	
1991 Q1	85 028	18 516	11 357	29 873	25 966	-1 493	139 374	30 231	169 605	33 053			18 742	1 623	
Q2	88 911	19 465	11 721	31 186	22 385	-844	141 638	33 753	175 391	35 507			20 733	1 480	
Q3	93 858	19 658	11 875	31 533	23 717	-374	148 734	34 172	182 906	36 610			22 408	1 291	
Q4	97 260	19 446	12 167	31 613	24 466	-2 358	150 981	35 992	186 973	35 605			22 933	1 601	
1992 Q1	89 103	20 189	12 230	32 419	24 779	-1 098	145 203	32 974	178 177	35 185			21 118	1 821	
Q2	93 279	21 049	12 343	33 392	21 164	-313	147 522	34 917	182 439	37 462			20 995	1 538	
Q3	98 071	20 532	12 442	32 974	22 741	580	154 366	34 412	188 778	37 829			22 350	1 421	
Q4	101 959	20 728	12 723	33 451	24 057	-1 161	158 306	37 948	196 254	38 979			23 121	1 632	
1993 Q1	94 442	20 836	12 856	33 692	24 860	-841	152 153	38 128	190 281	39 896			21 704	2 192	
Q2	98 551	22 456	12 324	34 780	20 950	572	154 853	38 356	193 209	41 856			21 935	1 719	
Q3	104 667	22 392	12 277	34 669	23 255	660	163 251	39 989	203 240	42 959			23 383	1 323	
Q4	108 211	22 428	12 497	34 925	24 082	-58	167 160	41 491	208 651	41 731			24 218	2 251	
1994 Q1	100 728	23 034	12 521	35 555	25 676	-753	161 206	40 233	201 439	41 361			22 868	1 876	
Seasonally adjusted															
1989 Q1	79 717	15 165	9 354	24 519	25 853	1 189	131 278	28 759	160 037	34 402	-	**125 635**	19 569	1 457	**107 523**
Q2	81 185	15 470	9 470	24 940	25 828	916	132 869	29 669	162 538	35 356	-	**127 182**	20 063	1 533	**108 652**
Q3	82 213	16 270	9 728	25 998	26 295	1 498	136 004	30 820	166 824	36 749	-	**130 075**	20 074	1 473	**111 474**
Q4	84 248	16 389	9 950	26 339	26 559	-18	137 128	32 238	169 366	36 301	-	**133 065**	20 274	1 319	**114 110**
1990 Q1	85 928	16 732	10 166	26 898	27 283	235	140 344	33 115	173 459	38 050	-	**135 409**	20 718	1 393	**116 084**
Q2	86 179	17 357	10 549	27 906	27 084	364	141 533	33 520	175 053	38 101	-	**136 952**	19 257	1 472	**119 167**
Q3	87 138	17 778	10 924	28 702	26 607	402	142 849	33 112	175 961	36 258	-	**139 703**	19 222	1 501	**121 982**
Q4	88 282	18 241	11 187	29 428	25 802	-2 119	141 393	33 537	174 930	35 876	-	**139 054**	19 101	1 700	**121 653**
1991 Q1	89 105	18 562	11 389	29 951	24 790	-938	142 908	31 973	174 881	34 323	-88	**140 470**	19 298	1 487	**122 659**
Q2	90 779	19 364	11 733	31 097	24 314	-1 983	144 207	33 579	177 786	34 708	-109	**142 969**	21 586	1 477	**122 860**
Q3	92 046	19 618	11 905	31 523	23 724	-1 708	145 585	34 356	179 941	35 765	-124	**144 052**	21 843	1 448	**123 657**
Q4	93 127	19 541	12 093	31 634	23 706	-440	148 027	34 240	182 267	35 979	-134	**146 154**	22 089	1 583	**125 648**
1992 Q1	93 611	20 221	12 260	32 481	23 440	-1 536	147 996	34 348	182 344	36 080	-108	**146 156**	21 781	1 601	**125 976**
Q2	94 923	20 850	12 347	33 197	23 102	-509	150 713	34 887	185 600	36 902	-41	**148 657**	21 732	1 577	**128 502**
Q3	96 152	20 506	12 473	32 979	22 842	435	152 408	34 580	186 988	36 864	17	**150 141**	21 832	1 618	**129 927**
Q4	97 726	20 921	12 658	33 579	23 357	-382	154 280	36 436	190 716	39 609	-120	**150 987**	22 239	1 616	**130 364**
1993 Q1	99 052	20 894	12 880	33 774	23 335	-455	155 706	39 135	194 841	41 262	-196	**153 383**	22 385	1 941	**132 939**
Q2	100 431	22 193	12 403	34 596	22 894	713	158 634	38 440	197 074	41 054	-230	**155 790**	22 777	1 881	**134 894**
Q3	102 304	22 387	12 244	34 631	23 233	-181	159 987	40 119	200 106	41 750	-256	**158 100**	22 815	1 845	**137 130**
Q4	104 084	22 638	12 427	35 065	23 685	256	163 090	40 270	203 360	42 376	-272	**160 712**	23 263	1 818	**139 267**
1994 Q1	105 522	23 074	12 521	35 595	24 154	-480	164 791	41 137	205 928	42 578	-294	**163 056**	23 602	1 816	**141 270**

1 Estimates are given to the nearest £ million but cannot be regarded as accurate to this degree.
2 This series is affected by the abolition of domestic rates and the introduction of the community charge.
3 Quarterly alignment adjustment included in this series. For description of adjustment see notes.

Data in this table update those contained in CSO Blue Book tables 1.2 and 1.3.

From: UKEA Table A2

NATIONAL ACCOUNTS (GDP)

4.4 Gross domestic product: by category of expenditure[1]

£ million

		General government final consumption				Value of physical increase in stocks and work in progress[3]						Statistical discrep-ancy (expend-iture)	Gross domestic product at market prices	less Taxes on expend-iture	Gross domestic product at factor cost
	Con-sumers' expend-iture[2]	Central govern ment	Local author-ities	Total	Gross domeslic fixed capital formation		Total	Exports of goods and services	Total final expend iture	less imports of goods and services					
Revalued at 1990 prices															
1984	266 486	66 146	39 030	105 177	78 270	1 764	450 949	103 019	553 528	103 282	677	**451 131**	59 064	**392 067**
1985	276 742	66 241	38 856	105 097	81 575	1 336	464 316	109 163	573 567	105 957	-	**468 071**	60 310	**407 844**
1986	295 622	67 277	39 547	106 824	83 685	1 199	487 330	114 047	601 377	113 255	-	**488 122**	63 908	**424 214**
1987	311 234	67 122	40 736	107 858	92 260	1 731	513 083	120 607	633 690	122 075	-	**511 615**	67 798	**443 817**
1988	334 591	67 588	41 024	108 612	104 726	5 532	553 461	121 197	674 658	137 443		**537 215**	71 469	**465 746**
1989	345 406	68 836	41 303	110 139	110 503	3 669	569 717	126 836	696 553	147 615	-	**548 938**	72 712	**476 226**
1990	347 527	70 108	42 826	112 934	106 776	-1 118	566 119	133 284	699 403	148 285	-	**551 118**	72 232	**478 886**
1991	339 993	71 950	43 847	115 797	96 265	-4 722	547 333	132 114	679 447	140 248	430	**538 769**	71 049	**467 720**
1992	339 967	72 542	43 624	116 166	94 993	-1 773	549 353	136 103	685 456	149 056	-228	**536 172**	70 298	**465 874**
1993	348 499	73 861	42 494	116 355	95 332	335	560 521	140 328	700 849	153 274	-833	**546 742**	71 821	**474 921**
Unadjusted															
1989 Q1	82 250	17 456	10 337	27 793	29 437	919	140 399	30 128	170 527	35 578			17 856	
Q2	84 317	16 602	10 272	26 874	26 040	1 976	139 207	31 336	170 543	37 701			17 373	
Q3	88 548	17 279	10 276	27 555	27 212	1 136	144 451	31 653	176 104	38 327			18 646	
Q4	90 291	17 499	10 418	27 917	27 814	-362	145 660	33 719	179 379	36 009			18 837	
1990 Q1	83 417	17 941	10 509	28 450	28 621	-112	140 376	32 064	172 440	36 640			17 865	
Q2	85 222	17 212	10 679	27 891	25 049	578	138 740	33 230	171 970	38 092			17 576	
Q3	88 806	17 204	10 734	27 938	26 222	457	143 423	32 727	176 150	37 820			18 335	
Q4	90 082	17 751	10 904	28 655	26 864	-2 041	143 580	35 263	178 843	35 733			18 456	
1991 Q1	82 263	17 975	10 971	28 946	25 835	-1 431	135 613	30 352	165 965	33 594			17 401	
Q2	82 616	17 956	10 952	28 908	22 150	-762	132 912	33 230	166 142	35 500			16 900	
Q3	86 463	18 001	10 907	28 908	23 739	-265	138 845	33 173	172 018	35 952			17 949	
Q4	88 651	18 018	11 017	29 035	24 541	-2 264	139 963	35 359	175 322	35 202			18 799	
1992 Q1	80 531	18 333	11 031	29 364	25 271	-1 023	134 143	32 382	166 525	35 357			17 266	
Q2	82 676	18 439	10 849	29 288	21 690	-265	133 389	34 001	167 390	37 878			16 776	
Q3	86 952	17 815	10 811	28 626	23 355	664	139 597	33 591	173 188	38 529			17 724	
Q4	89 808	17 955	10 933	28 888	24 677	-1 149	142 224	36 129	178 353	37 292			18 532	
1993 Q1	82 335	17 748	11 026	28 774	25 553	-850	135 812	33 867	169 679	36 735			17 445	
Q2	84 263	18 669	10 489	29 158	21 413	675	135 509	34 207	169 716	38 337			17 206	
Q3	89 461	18 719	10 487	29 206	23 662	593	142 922	35 327	178 249	39 618			18 163	
Q4	92 440	18 725	10 492	29 217	24 704	-83	146 278	36 927	183 205	38 584			19 007	
1994 Q1	85 255	18 997	10 517	29 514	26 684	-738	140 715	35 640	176 355	38 268			18 075	
Seasonally adjusted															
1989 Q1	85 847	17 023	10 259	27 282	28 343	953	142 425	31 496	173 921	37 133	-	**136 788**	18 120	**118 668**
Q2	86 472	16 925	10 260	27 185	27 551	1 485	142 693	31 000	173 693	36 468	-	**137 225**	18 327	**118 898**
Q3	86 243	17 545	10 378	27 923	27 449	1 345	142 960	31 759	174 719	37 350	-	**137 369**	18 239	**119 130**
Q4	86 844	17 343	10 406	27 749	27 160	-114	141 639	32 581	174 220	36 664	-	**137 556**	18 026	**119 530**
1990 Q1	86 992	17 547	10 443	27 990	27 628	27	142 637	33 259	175 896	37 630	-	**138 266**	18 112	**120 154**
Q2	87 409	17 484	10 673	28 157	27 124	547	143 237	33 264	176 501	37 487	-	**139 014**	18 433	**120 581**
Q3	86 778	17 448	10 824	28 272	26 397	-133	141 314	33 110	174 424	36 881	-	**137 543**	18 029	**119 514**
Q4	86 348	17 629	10 886	28 515	25 627	-1 559	138 931	33 651	172 582	36 287	-	**136 295**	17 658	**118 637**
1991 Q1	85 834	17 902	10 917	28 819	24 669	-1 078	138 244	31 932	170 176	34 908	-84	**135 184**	17 707	**117 477**
Q2	84 806	18 086	10 944	29 030	24 063	-1 692	136 207	33 159	169 366	34 726	-104	**134 536**	17 657	**116 879**
Q3	64 712	18 039	10 990	29 029	23 750	-1 535	135 956	33 475	169 431	34 923	-117	**134 391**	17 715	**116 676**
Q4	64 641	17 923	10 996	28 919	23 783	-417	136 926	33 548	170 474	35 691	-125	**134 658**	17 970	**116 688**
1992 Q1	84 328	18 220	10 976	29 196	23 934	-1 313	136 145	33 608	169 753	36 237	-99	**133 417**	17 478	**115 939**
Q2	84 697	18 427	10 838	29 265	23 645	-540	137 067	34 014	171 081	37 423	-37	**133 621**	17 542	**116 079**
Q3	85 204	17 907	10 898	28 805	23 457	487	137 953	33 917	171 870	37 492	15	**134 393**	17 608	**116 785**
Q4	85 738	17 988	10 912	28 900	23 957	-407	138 188	34 564	172 752	37 904	-107	**134 741**	17 670	**117 071**
1993 Q1	86 015	17 633	11 026	28 659	23 994	-175	138 493	34 895	173 388	38 053	-173	**135 162**	17 645	**117 517**
Q2	86 494	18 733	10 489	29 222	23 407	532	139 655	34 393	174 048	37 660	-202	**136 186**	18 085	**118 101**
Q3	87 495	18 789	10 487	29 276	23 671	-179	140 263	35 420	175 683	38 262	-223	**137 198**	17 994	**119 204**
Q4	88 495	18 706	10 492	29 198	24 260	157	142 110	35 620	177 730	39 299	-235	**138 196**	18 097	**120 099**
1994 Q1	89 007	18 851	10 517	29 368	24 758	449	142 684	36 423	179 107	39 612	-252	**139 243**	18 331	**120 912**

1 Estimates are given to the nearest £ million but cannot be regarded as accurate to this degree.
2 Quarterly alignment adjustment included in this series. For description of adjustment see notes.
3 *Represents* Taxes on expenditure *less* Subsidies, both valued at 1990 prices.

Data in this table update those contained in CSO Blue Book tables 1.2 and 1.3.

From: UKEA Table A2

Key Data 94, © Crown copyright 1994

4.5 Gross domestic product at factor cost: by category of income[1]

£ million

	Income from employment	Gross trading profits of companies [2 3 4 5]	Gross trading surplus of public corporations [3 5]	Gross trading surplus of general government enterprises[3]	Other income[6]	Total domestic income[7]	less Stock appreciation	Statistical discrepancy (income)	Gross domestic product at factor cost
At current prices									
1984	181 406	43 852	8 511	-117	50 344	283 996	4 513	1 170	280 653
1985	196 858	51 146	7 262	265	55 109	310 640	2 738	-	307 902
1986	212 380	47 339	8 213	155	62 020	330 107	1 835	-	328 272
1987	229 832	59 068	6 993	-75	69 584	365 402	4 727	-	360 675
1988	255 634	63 997	7 554	-32	80 650	407 803	6 375	-	401 428
1989	283 454	66 464	6 528	199	92 175	448 820	7 061	-	441 759
1990	312 358	64 748	3 801	12	104 098	485 017	6 131	-	478 886
1991	328 257	61 409	1 809	-36	105 917	497 356	2 522	-10	494 824
1992	341 189	63 686	2 056	188	110 071	517 190	2 216	-205	514 769
1993	350 239	78 583	2 986	274	115 000	547 082	2 308	-544	544 230
Unadjusted									
1989 Q1	67 684	16 320	2 044	110	22 005	108 163	2 013		
Q2	69 934	16 382	1 513	-53	22 790	110 566	2 214		
Q3	71 701	16 216	1 167	61	23 404	112 549	1 149		
Q4	74 135	17 546	1 804	81	23 976	117 542	1 685		
1990 Q1	75 236	15 942	1 359	32	25 241	117 810	1 943		
Q2	77 568	15 834	843	-12	26 046	120 279	1 624		
Q3	79 230	16 364	593	43	26 346	122 576	1 797		
Q4	80 324	16 608	1 006	-51	26 465	124 352	767		
1991 Q1	80 562	15 009	542	-6	26 170	122 277	1 066		
Q2	81 599	14 958	483	-73	26 480	123 447	998		
Q3	82 383	14 012	343	39	26 534	123 311	211		
Q4	83 713	17 430	441	4	26 733	128 321	247		
1992 Q1	84 542	14 737	312	18	27 088	126 697	1 103		
Q2	85 192	15 220	604	30	27 537	128 583	549		
Q3	85 565	14 806	462	89	27 727	128 649	-4		
Q4	85 890	18 923	678	51	27 719	133 261	568		
1993 Q1	86 358	17 910	596	2	28 293	133 159	1 063		
Q2	87 150	18 495	805	112	28 719	135 281	690		
Q3	88 009	18 628	565	91	28 917	136 210	99		
Q4	88 722	23 550	1 020	69	29 071	142 432	456		
1994 Q1	90 131	21 796	246	-109	29 483	141 547	634		
Seasonally adjusted									
1989 Q1	68 196	17 282	1 800	110	22 058	109 446	1 923	-	107 523
Q2	69 955	16 444	1 676	-53	22 756	110 778	2 126	-	108 652
Q3	71 655	16 093	1 569	61	23 391	112 769	1 295	-	111 474
Q4	73 648	16 645	1 483	81	23 970	115 827	1 717	-	114 110
1990 Q1	75 746	15 594	1 090	32	25 324	117 786	1 702	-	116 084
Q2	77 586	16 002	1 046	-12	25 964	120 586	1 419	-	119 167
Q3	79 196	17 527	972	43	26 323	124 061	2 079	-	121 982
Q4	79 830	15 625	693	-51	26 487	122 584	931	-	121 653
1991 Q1	81 062	15 597	557	-6	26 269	123 479	810	-10	122 659
Q2	81 601	15 389	447	-73	26 341	123 705	837	8	122 860
Q3	82 365	14 812	421	39	26 511	124 148	489	-2	123 657
Q4	83 229	15 611	384	4	26 796	126 024	386	10	125 648
1992 Q1	84 775	14 422	371	18	27 151	126 737	853	92	125 976
Q2	85 181	15 798	531	30	27 387	128 927	367	-58	128 502
Q3	85 550	16 601	543	89	27 683	130 466	319	-220	129 927
Q4	85 683	16 865	611	51	27 850	131 060	677	-19	130 364
1993 Q1	86 561	18 268	640	2	28 335	133 806	751	-116	132 939
Q2	87 142	18 995	755	112	28 575	135 579	553	-132	134 894
Q3	88 009	20 042	637	91	28 869	137 648	373	-145	137 130
Q4	88 527	21 278	954	69	29 221	140 049	631	-151	139 267
1994 Q1	90 333	21 937	285	-109	29 514	141 960	573	-117	141 270

1 Estimates are given to the nearest £ million but cannot be regarded as accurate to this degree.
2 Quarterly alignment adjustment included in this series. For description of adjustment see Notes.
3 Before providing for depreciation and stock appreciation.
4 Including financial institutions.
5 Figures reflect privatisations.
6 Income from rent and from self-employment and the imputed charge for the consumption of non-trading capital.
7 The sum of the factor incomes before deducting Stock appreciation.

Data in this table update those contained in CSO Blue Book table 1.4.

From: UKEA Table A3

NATIONAL ACCOUNTS (GDP)

4.6 Index numbers of output at constant factor cost[1]

1990 = 100

	Production						Service industries					Gross domestic product at factor cost[2]	Gross domestic product excl. oil and gas extraction
	Agric-ulture, fores-try, and fishing	Mining & quarrying inc oil & gas extrac-tion	Manuf-acturing (revised defini-tion)	Elec-tricity, gas and water supply	Total	Construc-tion	Distrib-ution hotels and catering; repairs	Transport storage communi-cation	Financial and business services	Govern-ment and other services	Total		
1990 Weights	19	22	237	22	281	72	142	84	186	217	629	1000	983
1984	100.6	117.7	82.2	71.3	83.4	72.8	78.0	77.2	79.2	90.9	82.7	81.9	80.9
1985	95.3	129.4	84.5	86.5	88.0	73.0	81.3	80.3	82.4	92.3	85.2	85.2	84.2
1986	95.5	133.8	85.6	95.1	90.1	76.0	85.8	83.7	87.2	94.0	88.8	88.6	87.8
1987	93.5	134.1	89.6	97.6	93.7	84.9	91.4	89.6	90.9	96.6	92.8	92.7	91.9
1988	92.1	123.4	95.9	97.7	98.2	92.3	96.9	94.2	96.6	99.1	97.2	97.3	96.8
1989	96.7	104.3	100.2	97.3	100.3	97.6	100.8	99.1	97.8	99.6	99.3	99.4	99.4
1 990	100.0	100.0	100.0	100.0	100.0	100.0	100.0	100.0	100.0	100.0	100.0	100.0	100.0
1991	103.9	101.0	94.7	105.9	96.0	92.1	95.3	97.3	100.0	100.5	98.8	97.7	97.6
1992	108.7	104.8	93.9	105.4	95.6	86.9	93.9	99.0	99.3	101.3	98.7	97.3	97.1
1993	104.4	115.0	95.4	108.5	97.9	85.3	96.8	102.3	100.9	102.6	100.7	99.2	98.7
Seasonally adjusted													
1989 Q1	95.9	102.7	100.2	94.1	99.9	96.4	100.4	97.7	97.3	99.9	99.0	99.1	99.1
Q2	95.4	99.2	99.9	99.7	99.9	98.0	100.8	98.6	97.7	99.7	99.2	99.3	99.4
Q3	98.3	107.0	100.2	97.5	100.5	97.6	100.9	100.1	97.7	99.2	99.3	99.5	99.4
Q4	97.2	108.4	100.4	97.9	100.8	98.6	100.9	100.0	98.6	99.4	99.6	99.8	99.7
1990 Q1	97.8	103.3	100.6	94.1	100.3	100.7	101.6	101.2	100.0	99.7	100.4	100.4	100.3
Q2	99.3	108.8	101.1	100.2	101.6	101.0	101.0	100.3	100.2	100.0	100.3	100.7	100.5
Q3	100.6	93.4	100.1	102.7	99.8	100.4	99.7	99.3	99.7	100.1	99.8	99.8	100.0
Q4	102.2	94.5	98.3	103.0	98.3	97.9	97.8	99.2	100.1	100.2	99.5	99.1	99.2
1991 Q1	103.7	98.7	96.2	104.9	97.1	94.5	96.8	95.9	100.0	100.1	98.8	98.1	98.1
Q2	104.8	95.1	94.6	110.2	95.9	92.7	95.2	97.2	99.9	100.4	98.7	97.6	97.7
Q3	103.0	103.4	94.0	102.6	95.4	91.4	95.0	97.5	100.1	100.7	98.8	97.5	97.3
Q4	104.1	106.6	93.8	106.1	95.8	89.8	94.3	98.4	99.9	101.0	98.8	97.5	97.3
1992 Q1	106.7	103.4	93.4	103.9	95.0	88.3	93.2	98.7	98.9	101.1	98.3	96.8	96.7
Q2	108.4	99.8	93.8	102.3	94.9	87.1	93.8	98.7	99.0	101.2	98.5	97.0	96.9
Q3	110.2	105.6	94.2	106.2	96.0	86.6	94.1	98.9	99.7	101.3	98.9	97.5	97.3
Q4	109.4	110.5	94.2	109.2	96.6	85.6	94.6	99.8	99.5	101.8	99.2	97.8	97.5
1993 Q1	106.2	105.8	95.1	103.2	96.6	85.1	95.5	100.4	100.0	102.1	99.8	98.2	97.9
Q2	102.2	108.8	95.3	105.8	97.2	85.1	96.2	101.0	100.7	102.4	100.3	98.6	98.3
Q3	104.7	118.2	95.4	111.2	98.4	84.9	97.5	103.0	101.2	102.8	101.2	99.6	99.0
Q4	104.5	127.1	95.7	113.9	99.6	85.9	97.9	104.7	101.7	103.0	101.7	100.3	99.6
1994 Q1	104.1	130.0	97.1	106.4	100.3	86.8	99.1	105.1	102.8	103.1	102.4	101.0	100.1

1 Estimates cannot be regarded as accurate to the last digit shown.
2 Embraces an implicit statistical discrepancy compared with the sum of the previous columns, because GDP takes account of other information based on incomes and expenditures.

Data in this table update those contained in CSO Blue Book tables 1.6 and 2.5.

From: UKEA Table A4

Key Data 94, © Crown copyright 1994

Definitions and sources

A new presentation of the measure of broad money was introduced in May 1987. Among other changes, M4 was introduced to cover the sterling deposit liabilities of banks and building societies for the rest of the private sector, and holdings by the latter of notes and coin.

The public sector borrowing requirement (PSBR) indicates the extent to which the public sector borrows from other sectors of the economy and overseas to finance the balance of expenditure and receipts arising from its various activities.

A much wider range of financial series is shown in *Financial Statistics* monthly and the *Bank of England Quarterly Bulletin*. More detailed information is given in the supplementary notes to the *Monthly Digest of Statistics* and in the *Financial Statistics Explanatory Handbook*. For other sources see:

Guide to Official Statistics, 1990 edition (200 pages approximately, fully indexed) HMSO.

Financial Statistics HMSO.

5.1   Monetary aggregates

£ million

	Amount outstanding					
	'Narrow' money		'Broad' money			
	M0–the wide monetary base		Retail deposits and cash in M4		M4	
	Not seasonally adjusted	Seasonally adjusted	Not seasonally adjusted	Seasonally adjusted	Not seasonally adjusted	Seasonally adjusted
1989	19 006	17 825	280 737	279 488	423 366	422 337
1990	19 491	18 299	310 628	309 339	474 274	473 561
1991	20 085	18 854	336 766	335 693	502 086	501 624
1992	20 581	19 360	374 055	373 144	519 279	519 069
1993	21 738	20 496	395 491	394 818	549 219	548 832
1991 Q1	18 178	18 454	319 140	318 079	482 972	482 036
Q2	18 585	18 646	326 842	325 210	493 123	489 728
Q3	18 751	18 721	332 435	331 570	498 057	496 206
Q4	20 085	18 854	336 766	335 693	502 086	501 624
1992 Q1	18 411	18 849	341 293	339 921	507 582	506 571
Q2	18 847	18 947	344 449	342 838	515 320	512 004
Q3	19 230	19 152	347 004	346 650	517 758	516 314
Q4	20 581	19 360	374 055	373 144	519 279	519 069
1993 Q1	19 305	19 666	378 583	377 108	525 814	524 710
Q2	19 835	19 866	384 200	382 657	532 193	529 393
Q3	20 267	20 204	387 528	387 415	538 032	537 010
Q4	21 738	20 496	395 491	394 818	549 219	548 832
1994 Q1	20 572	20 764	401 485	399 985	557 676	556 535
1993 Mar	19 305	19 666	378 583	377 108	525 814	524 710
Apr	19 919	19 920	380 599	379 609	527 036	526 335
May	19 663	19 799	383 727	382 142	530 071	528 633
Jun	19 835	19 866	384 200	382 657	532 193	529 393
Jul	20 144	20 080	384 815	384 266	534 277	532 688
Aug	20 337	20 162	384 716	385 636	534 851	535 062
Sep	20 267	20 204	387 528	387 415	538 032	537 010
Oct	20 156	20 251	389 033	389 471	541 485	540 969
Nov	20 294	20 294	390 745	391 563	543 082	544 050
Dec	21 738	20 496	395 491	394 818	549 219	548 832
1994 Jan	20 615	20 511	393 114	396 052	546 096	550 479
Feb	20 291	20 701	395 891	398 026	549 469	553 559
Mar	20 572	20 764	401 485	399 985	557 676	556 535

1 Equals M2 from December 1992.

Source: Bank of England

From: Monthly Digest of Statistics, May 1994, Table 17.4

5.2 Public sector borrowing requirement[1]

£ million

	Total		Contributions by			Financed by:				
						Banks and building societies/Overseas sector			Other private sector	
						External finance				
	Not seasonally adjusted	Seasonally adjusted[2]	Central government (own account)[3]	Local authorities[4]	Public corporations[4]	Borrowing in sterling from banks	Foreign currency borrowing from banks	Other external finance	Notes and coin	Other
1990	-2 116	-2 454	-1 109	3 903	-4 910	297	-20	-4 267	-101	608
1991	7 704	7 561	6 588	1 878	-762	-944	36	3 277	451	4 154
1992	28 890	28 393	33 706	-5 562	746	675	4 548	5 049	1 080	19 107
1993	43 078	42 959	46 155	-2 836	-241	4 465	603	13 673	958	..
Financial years										
1990/91	-452	-452	-2 916	3 451	-987	-335	115	-2 185	711	907
1991/92	13 879	13 879	11 735	1 685	459	1 048	30	4 663	-590	7 798
1992/93	36 569	36 569	42 368	-5 843	44	3 689	5 211	3 082	799	24 335
1993/94	45 923	45 923	47 845	-2 738	816	..	..	..	..	..
1992 Q1	3 593	6 555	1 737	1 165	691	-257	-95	1 620	-575	2 740
Q2	10 614	5 426	10 467	52	95	697	-116	1 370	285	8 120
Q3	7 679	7 154	9 096	-1 157	-260	-5 069	4 057	6 330	72	3 252
Q4	7 004	9 258	12 406	-5 622	220	5 304	702	-4 271	1 298	4 995
1993 Q1	11 272	14 731	10 399	884	-11	2 757	568	-347	856	7 968
Q2	13 369	8 001	13 022	-99	446	2 384	-183	3 415	381	7 709
Q3	10 766	10 344	12 144	-1 218	-160	-1 196	60	6 524	478	5 770
Q4	7 671	9 883	10 590	-2 403	-516	520	158	4 081	955	..
1994 Q1	14 117	17 695	12 089	982	1 046	..	..	..	..	..

1 For further details see *Financial Statistics* Tables I.IA, I0.IA and I0.IB.
2 Financial year constrained.
3 An increase in debt is shown positive.
4 Includes direct borrowing from central government.

Source: Central Statistical Office
From: Monthly Digest of Statistics, May1994, Table 17.2

5.3 Selected interest rates, exchange rates and security prices

	Selected retail banks' base rate	Average discount rate for 91 day Treasury bills	Inter-bank 3 months bid rate	Inter-bank 3 months offer rate	British government securities 20 years yield[1]	Sterling exchange rate index 1985=100	Exchange rate U S spot	Ordinary share price index[2]
1993 Apr	6.00	5.39	6.13	6.13	8.39	80.5	1.5683	1 393.70
May	6.00	5.25	5.84	5.91	8.60	80.4	1.5635	1 397.10
Jun	6.00	5.19	5.88	5.94	8.39	79.6	1.5005	1 419.94
Jul	6.00	5.09	5.88	5.94	7.96	81.3	1.4810	1 413.38
Aug	6.00	5.09	5.69	5.75	7.39	81.0	1.4883	1 498.55
Sep	6.00	5.19	5.88	5.91	7.18	80.8	1.4982	1 505.06
Oct	6.00	5.01	5.63	5.69	7.09	80.4	1.4882	1 544.80
Nov	5.50	4.81	5.31	5.34	7.06	81.0	1.4815	1 535.11
Dec	5.50	4.89	5.31	5.31	6.46	81.7	1.4780	1 628.88
1994 Jan	5.25	4.85	5.41	5.44	6.41	82.5	1.4990	1 710.35
Feb	5.25	4.71	5.19	5.19	6.83	81.0	1.4864	1 709.09
Mar	5.25	4.93	5.22	5.25	7.47	80.5	1.4845	1 619.80
Apr	5.25	4.85	5.19	5.19	7.83	80.0	1.5165	1 582.06

1 Average of working days.
2 Financial Times Actuaries share indices 10 April 1962 = 100. All classes (750 shares) index.

Source: Bank of England

From: Monthly Digest of Statistics, May 1994, Table 17.5

Key Data 94, © Crown copyright 1994

5.4   Selected financial statistics[1]

£ million

	National savings[2]	Building societies				Unit trusts	Net inflow into life assurance & super-annuation funds
		Deposits		Advances			
		Not seasonally adjusted	Seasonally adjusted	Not seasonally adjusted	Seasonally adjusted		
Amount outstanding							
31 Dec 1993	47 736	..		229 638		95 518	
Transactions							
1990	932	18 052		26 338	26 339	393	27 799
1991	2 254	17 890		22 203	22 203	2 770	28 979
1992	5 147	11 447		14 909	14 907	647	28 926
1993	3 055	9 298		11 139	11 138	9 135	..
1993 Q1	647	3 602	2 744	1 963	2 658	1 848	6 952
Q2	701	2 737	2 764	3 100	2 885	2 492	6 511
Q3	616	1 463	1 718	3 319	2 753	2 607	8 026
Q4	1 091	1 496	2 073	2 757	2 842	2 188	
1994 Q1	1 724	834	194	3 181	3 779	2 586	..
1993 Mar	242	1 140	1136	858	954	769	
Apr	277	1 264	947	1 049	984	967	
May	208	664	869	1 049	1 013	914	
Jun	216	809	948	1 002	888	611	
Jul	123	69	123	1 324	917	955	
Aug	232	416	924	858	789	981	
Sep	261	978	671	1 137	1 047	671	
Oct	447	496	797	1 031	1 015	867	
Nov	396	-268	660	864	781	426	
Dec	248	1 268	616	862	1 046	895	
1994 Jan	387	506	-151	940	1 062	490	
Feb	783	375	406	812	1 193	722	
Mar	554	-47	-61	1 429	1 524	1 374	

1 For further details see *Financal Statistics*, Tables 1.2E, 3.2B, 4.2A, 4.3A,4.3B,5.2D, 6.2A,10.5D.
2 Total administered by the Department for National Savings.
3 Monthly figures relate to calendar months.

Sources: Central Statistical Office;
Department for National Savings;
Building Societies Association;
Unit Trust Association;
Bank of England;
Department of Trade and Industry

From: Monthly Digest of Statistics, May 1994, Table 17.3

Continued overleaf

5.4 Selected financial statistics[1]
Continued

£ million

	Banks[3]						Narrower coverage Consumer credit		Broader coverage Consumer credit	
	UK private sector deposits			Lending to the private sector						
	Sterling			Sterling						
	Not seasonally adjusted	Seasonally adjusted	Other currencies	Not seasonally adjusted	Seasonally adjusted	Other currencies	Not seasonally adjusted	Seasonally adjusted	Not seasonally adjusted	Seasonally adjusted
Amount outstanding										
31 Dec 1993	345 965		57 612	416 291		76 565	32 096	31 646	52 379	52 032
Transactions										
1990	31 810		10 610	46 785		2 552	3 683		4 438	
1991	13 450		4 662	13 938		9 193	1 060		2 365	
1992	5 187		6 707	9 104		-2 599	364		368	
1993	17 541		5 186	12 355		7 416	2 934		2 209	
1993 Q1	3 576	4 142	381	5 535	4 031	153	-330	446	- 493	254
Q2	2 258	895	834	-1 764	699	2 429	691	547	601	426
Q3	4 326	4470	427	5 946	3 977	558	1 320	900	1 267	799
Q4	7 381	8034	3 544	2 638	3 648	4 276	1 253	1 046	834	722
1994 Q1	6 152	6 925	1 322	6 042	4 595	2 183	370	1 087	-28	709
1993 Mar	6 498		-1 014	4 026		-277	66	217		
Apr	-2 531		1 951	-3 285		1 512	320	199		
May	2 960		-677	-362		904	143	130		
Jun	1 829		-440	1 883		13	228	218		
Jul	316		1 691	361		-2 664	150	208		
Aug	949		154	2 043		1 313	607	236		
Sep	3 061		-1 418	3 542		1 909	563	456		
Oct	2 964		1 087	340		61	122	301		
Nov	3 562		1 131	2 171		3 802	345	320		
Dec	855		1 326	127		413	786	425		
1994 Jan	-1 861		-267	282		3 794	69	235		
Feb	2 485		880	-117		1 926	-102	336		
Mar	5 528		709	5 876		-3 537	403	516		

1 For further details see *Financial Statistics*, Tables 1.2E, 3.2B, 4.2A, 4.3A,4.3B,5.2D, 6.2A,10.5D.
2 Total administered by the Department for National Savings.
3 Monthly figures relate to calendar months.

Sources: Central Statistical Office;
Department for National Savings;
Building Societies Association;
Unit Trust Association;
Bank of England;
Department of Trade and Industry

From: Monthly Digest of Statistics, May 1994, Table 17.3

Key Data 94, © Crown copyright 1994

Definitions and sources

The object of the balance of payments accounts is to identify and record transactions between residents of the United Kingdom and residents overseas (non-residents) in a way that is suitable for analysing the economic relations between the UK economy and the rest of the world. In the UK balance of payments accounts, transactions are classified into main groups as follows:

Current account transactions cover exports and imports of goods and services, investment income and most transfers.

Transactions in UK external assets and liabilities cover inward and outward investment, transactions by banks in the United Kingdom, borrowing and lending overseas by other UK residents, drawings on and accruals to the official reserves, and other capital transactions.

The *current balance* shows whether the United Kingdom has had a surplus of income over expenditure; and, taken with capital transfers, it shows whether the United Kingdom has added to or consumed its net external assets in any period.

In concept every balance of payments transaction involves equal credit and debit entries, relating to the two halves of the transaction so that the accounts are analogous to a double-entry book-keeping system. For example an export of goods, recorded as positive, would be matched by a negative entry, which could be one of the following:

   (i)   an increase in the foreign assets (claims on non-residents) of the United Kingdom (eg an increase in UK residents' deposits with banks abroad);

   (ii)   a decrease in the United Kingdom's liabilities to non-residents (eg a fall in sterling deposits with UK banks);

or (iii)   in the case of a barter transaction, by imports of similar value.

Conversely imports of goods, recorded as negative, are likely to be matched by positive entries representing reductions in foreign assets held by the United Kingdom or increases in the United Kingdom's liabilities to non-residents.

Since the two entries made in respect of each transaction generally derived from separate sources and methods of estimation are neither complete nor precisely accurate, the two entries may not match each other precisely or may fall within different recording periods. In order to bring the total of all entries to zero an additional entry, the balancing item, is therefore included to reflect the sum of all these errors and omissions. The balancing item will include persistent elements, where certain types of transactions are not adequately covered in the accounts, and timing differences.

The balance of payments estimates are compiled from a large number of different sources and the degree of accuracy attained varies considerably between items. Errors are likely, to some extent, to offset each other in any particular year but where a balance is drawn between two aggregates and the balance is small in relation to the aggregates, such as the current balance, the proportionate error attached to the balance is liable to be very substantial.

Detailed notes and definitions relating to the balance of payments (including foreign trade) are given in the annual publication *United Kingdom Balance of Payments* (the CSO 'Pink Book').

The data in these tables are consistent with that published in the June 1994 Balance of Payments First Release. These data will be further revised upon publication of the 1994 edition of the Pink Book due to be published on 8 September.

For other sources see:

Guide to Official Statistics, 1990 edition (200 pages approximately, fully indexed) HMSO.

UK Balance of Payments, CSO 'Pink Book'.

Overseas Trade Statistics of the United Kingdom.

6.1   Summary balance of payments

£ million

	1983	1984	1985	1986	1987	1988	1989	1990	1991	1992	1993
CURRENT ACCOUNT											
Visible trade (balance)	-1 537	-5 336	-3 345	-9 559	-11 582	-21 480	-24 683	-18 809	-10 284	-13 406	-13 680
Invisibles (balance):											
Services	3 829	4 205	6 398	6 223	6 242	3 957	3 361	3 808	3 657	4 202	5 202
Interest, profits and dividends	2 830	4 344	2 296	4 622	3 757	4 424	3 388	1 630	320	3 774	2 703
Transfers	-1 593	-1 732	-3 111	-2 157	-3 400	-3 518	-4 578	-4 897	-1 345	-5 109	-5 106
Invisible balance	5 066	6 817	5 583	8 688	6 599	4 863	2 171	541	2 632	2 867	2 799
CURRENT BALANCE	3 529	1 482	2 238	-871	-4 983	-16 617	-22 512	-18 268	-7 652	-10 539	-10 881
Capital transfers	-	-	-	-	-	-	-	-	-	-	-
UK EXTERNAL ASSETS AND LIABILITIES											
Transactions in assets	-30 378	-32 188	-50 555	-92 489	-82 499	-58 458	-90 089	-82 187	-18 925	-84 075	-162 797
Transactions in liabilities	25 818	23 501	46 758	89 316	89 525	68 812	109 503	93 148	25 652	91 173	174 939
Net transactions	-4 562	-8 688	-3 797	-3 173	7 026	10 352	19 415	10 960	6 728	7 098	12 142
EEA loss on forward commitments	-	-	-	-	-	-	-	-	-	-	-
Allocation of Special Drawing Rights	-	-	-	-	-	-	-	-	-	-	-
Gold subscription IMF	-	-	-	-	-	-	-	-	-	-	-
Balancing item	1 033	7 206	1 559	4 044	-2 043	6 265	3 097	7 308	924	3 441	- 1 261

From: United Kingdom Balance of Payments 1993, Table 1.1

BALANCE OF PAYMENTS

6.2 Current account[1]

£ million

	1983	1984	1985	1986	1987	1988	1989	1990	1991	1992	1993
Credits											
Exports (f.o.b.)	60 700	70 265	77 991	72 627	79 153	80 346	92 154	101 718	103 413	107 047	120 839
Services											
General government	470	474	483	511	521	550	445	425	412	3 98	434
Private sector and public corporations											
Sea transport	2 834	2 987	2 986	2 859	2 932	3 276	3 522	3 444	3 351	3 440	3 834
Civil aviation	2 665	2 931	3 078	2 786	3 159	3 292	3 869	4 474	4 039	4 422	5 051
Travel	4 003	4 614	5 442	5 553	6 260	6 184	6 945	7 785	7 168	7 890	9 090
Financial and other services	9 208	10 361	12 061	13 549	1 4 372	13 625	14 551	15 438	15 765	17 054	18 716
Interest profits and dividends											
General government	765	817	738	765	949	1 459	1 949	1 812	1 764	1 566	1 413
Private sector and public corporations	41 685	50 804	51 270	46 576	47 053	55 091	72 029	77 215	75 075	67 099	70 814
Transfers											
General government	2 235	2 392	1 760	2 138	2 282	2 115	2 143	2 231	4 899	2 888	3 325
Private sector	1 528	1 652	1 775	1 732	1 666	1 715	1 750	1 800	1 900	1 975	2 050
Total invisibles	65 392	77 031	79 593	76 469	79 194	87 307	107 203	114 624	114 373	106 732	114 727
Total credits	126 092	147 296	157 584	149 096	158 347	167 653	199 357	216 342	217 786	213 779	235 566
Debits											
Imports (f.o.b.)	62 237	75 601	81 336	82 186	90 735	10 1826	11 6837	120 527	113 697	120 453	134 519
Services											
General government	1 522	1 655	1 781	1 920	2 141	2351	2699	2784	2 808	2 546	2332
Private sector and public corporations											
Sea transport	3 671	3 610	3 515	3 323	3 219	3 517	3 779	3 756	3 634	3 837	4 069
Civil aviation	2 363	2 676	2 877	3 194	3 775	4 203	4 397	4 769	4 423	4 969	5 549
Travel	4 090	4 663	4 871	6 083	7 280	8 216	9 357	9 916	9 834	11 244	12780
Financial and other services	3 705	4 558	4 608	4 515	4 587	4 683	5 739	6 533	6 379	6 406	7 193
Interest, profits and dividends											
General government	1 188	1 344	1 491	1 675	2 046	2 329	2 512	2 242	1 986	2 860	3 014
Private sector and public corporations	38 429	45 933	48 221	41 044	42 199	49 797	68 078	75 155	74 533	6 2031	66 510
Transfers											
General government	4 165	4 491	5 187	4 371	5 559	5 363	6 421	6 828	5 944	7 722	8 161
Private sector	1 191	1 283	1 459	1 656	1 789	1 985	2 050	2 100	2 200	2 250	2 320
Total invisibles	60 326	70 213	74 010	67 781	72 595	82 444	105 032	114 083	111 741	103 865	111 928
Total debits	122 563	145 814	155 346	149 967	163 330	184 270	221 869	234 610	225 438	224 318	246 447
Balances											
Visible balance	-1 537	-5 336	-3 345	-9 559	- 11 582	-21 480	-24 683	-18 809	-10 284	- 13 406	-13 680
Services											
General government	-1 052	-1 181	-1 298	-1 409	- 1 620	-1 801	-2 254	-2 359	-2 396	- 2 148	-1 898
Private sector and public corporations											
Sea transport	-837	-623	-529	-464	- 287	-241	-257	-312	-283	- 397	-235
Civil aviation	302	255	201	408	- 616	-911	-528	-295	-384	- 547	-498
Travel	-87	-49	571	-530	- 1 020	-2 032	-2 412	-2 131	-2 666	- 3 354	-3 690
Financial and other services	5 503	5 803	7 453	9 034	9 785	8 942	8 812	8 905	9 386	10 648	11 523
Interest, profits and dividends											
General government	424	-527	-753	-910	- 1 097	-870	-563	-430	-222	- 1 294	-1 601
Private sector and public corporations	3 255	4 871	3 049	5 532	4 854	5 294	3 951	2 060	542	5 068	4 304
Transfers											
General government	-1 930	-2 099	-3 427	-2 233	-3 277	-3 248	-4 278	-4 597	-1 045	- 4 834	-4 836
Private sector	337	368	316	76	- 123	-270	-300	-300	-300	- 275	-270
Invisibles balance	5 066	6 817	5 583	8 688	6 599	4 863	2 171	541	2 632	2 867	2 799
Of which: Private sector and public corporations: Services and IPD	8 136	10 257	10 745	13 164	12 716	11 052	9 566	8 227	6 595	11 418	11 404
Current balance	3 529	1 482	2 238	-871	- 4 983	-16 617	-22 512	-18 268	-7 652	- 10 539	-10 881

From: United Kingdom Balance of Payments, 1993, Table 1.3

Key Data 94, © Crown copyright 1994

6.3 Summary of transactions in UK external assets and liabilities (Capital account of the United Kingdom with the overseas sector)

£ million

	1983	1984	1985	1986	1987	1988	1989	1990	1991	1992	1993
Transactions in external assets of the UK (increase in assets shown negative)											
Direct investment overseas by UK residents	-5 417	-6 042	-8 430	-11 649	-19 147	-20 863	-21 503	-10 544	-8 841	-11 074	-17 111
Portfolio investment in overseas securities by UK residents	-7 350	-9 755	-16 692	-22 542	5 418	-11 225	-36 341	-16 470	-29 240	-33 338	-94 611
Lending etc to overseas residents by UK banks	-18 443	-14 359	-22 024	-53 714	-50 393	-19 691	-28 611	-41 230	32 229	-25 389	6 056
Deposits and lending overseas by UK residents other than banks and general government											
Transactions with banks abroad	863	-3 213	-1 305	3 094	-5 291	-4 026	-9 553	-9 023	-4 642	-5 739	-10 096
Other assets	-161	1 015	384	1 909	-278	993	1 352	-3 821	-4 856	-9 260	-45 724
Official reserves	607	908	-1 758	-2 891	-12 012	-2 761	5 440	-76	-2 679	1 407	-701
Other external assets of central government	-478	-743	-730	-509	-796	-887	-873	-1 025	-894	-682	-610
Total transactions in assets of											
General government	129	165	-2 488	-3 401	-12 808	-3 648	4 567	-1 101	-3 573	725	-1 311
Public corporations	47	-223	370	-121	-21	-33	-59	-48	-38	-73	-76
UK banks	-21 232	-21 402	-33 347	-62 989	-9 450	-20 972	-35 866	-47 828	24 444	-39 818	-30 438
UK non-bank private sector	-9 322	-10 728	-15 091	-25 979	-20 219	33 807	-58 731	-33 212	-39 757	-44 907	-130 973
Total	-30 378	-32 188	-50 555	-92 489	-82 499	-58 458	-90 089	-82 187	-18 925	-84 075	-162 797
Transactions in UK liabilities to overseas residents (increase in liabilities shown positive)											
Direct investment in the UK by overseas residents	3 386	-181	4 504	5 837	9 449	12 006	18 567	18 520	9 032	9 510	8 782
Portfolio investment in the UK by overseas residents	1 701	1 288	9 773	12 081	22 233	16 533	16 079	7 724	19 230	21 584	39 411
Borrowing etc from overseas residents by UK banks	21 293	24 139	29 042	66 868	52 151	34 088	44 854	47 568	-24 200	23 744	23 295
Borrowing from overseas by UK residents other than banks and general government											
Transactions with banks abroad	38	-2 263	2 682	3 786	2 446	3 720	6 208	9 840	13 527	7 031	16 224
Other liabilities	-15	558	732	568	1 414	1 635	20 975	8 799	10 392	30 559	90 453
Other external liabilities of general government	-584	-41	24	177	1 830	832	2 822	699	-2 329	-1 254	-3 224
Total transactions in liabilities of											
General government	347	583	3 235	3 420	6 302	2 038	1 121	-3 589	5 666	7 072	12 945
Public corporations	-46	-260	-51	-28	-247	-277	-2 075	-81	-52	-46 9	-27
UK private sector	25 517	23 179	43 574	85 926	83 470	67 053	110 459	96 819	20 039	84 570	162 023
Total	25 818	23 501	46 758	89 316	89 525	68 812	109 503	93 148	25 652	91 173	174 939
Of which: identified liabilities constituting overseas authorities' exchange reserves in sterling	981	1 308	1 577	33	4 577	2 314	903	1 639	-2 172	744	4 447
Net transactions in assets and liabilities of											
General government	474	746	747	18	-6 506	-1 610	5 686	-4 690	2 093	7 797	11 634
Public corporations	-	-484	319	-150	-269	-311	-2 134	-129	-89	-542	-103
UK private sector	-5 037	-8 952	-4 863	-3 042	13 801	12 274	15 862	15 779	4 725	-155	612
Total net	-4 562	-8 688	-3 797	-3 173	7 026	10 352	19 415	10 960	6 728	7 098	12 142
Allocation of Special Drawing Rights to the UK by the IMF	-	-	-	-	-	-	-	-	-	-	-

From: United Kingdom Balance of Payments, 1993, Table 7.1

6.4 UK net external assets by sector[1]

£ million

	1983	1984	1985	1986	1987	1988	1989	1990	1991	1992	1993
ASSETS less LIABILITIES											
General government	6 938	7 616	5 324	6 604	10 943	11 543	8 342	10 959	9 442	-46	-15 044
Public corporations	-3 586	-3 533	-3 163	-3 188	-2 261	-2 025	-7	132	252	719	808
Private sector	52 212	75 642	70 247	96 339	53 870	55 864	50 192	-11 793	-5 235	19 070	36 963
Total	55 565	79 725	72 408	99 754	62 551	65 382	58 527	-702	4 459	19 742	22 727

1 Because of the many inconsistencies in valuing the component series, and the omission of certain assets and liabilities which are unidentifiable, these estimates are not an exact measure of the UK's external debtor/ creditor position.

From: United Kingdom Balance of Payments, 1993, Table 1.2

As a European power, Britain is concerned first of all with prosperity and security of this area of the world.

The main instrument for achieving European prosperity is the European Community, which is an association of 12 democratic nations - Belgium, Britain, Denmark, France, Germany, Greece, the Irish Republic, Italy, Luxembourg, the Netherlands, Portugal and Spain.

The British Government is strongly in favour of enlarging the Community to include other democratic nations in Europe. In early 1993 accession negotiations were launched with Austria, Finland, Norway and Sweden. A target date of 1 January 1995 has been set for accession.

Britain regards the Community as a means of strengthening democracy and reinforcing political stability in Europe, and of increasing the collective strength of member states in international negotiations. The Government wants Britain to be at the heart of a Community in which member states work effectively together by pooling their ideas and resources for shared purposes, provided that such objectives cannot be achieved by member states acting on their own.

The Community had its origins in the resolve by Western European nations, particularly France and Germany, not to allow wars to break out again between themselves. The Rome Treaty defined Community aims as the harmonious development of economic activities, a continuous and balanced economic expansion and an accelerated rise in the standard of living. These objectives were to be achieved by the creation of a common internal market and progressive harmonisation of economic policies involving:

> the elimination of customs duties between member states;

> free movement of goods, people, services and capital; a common commercial policy towards other countries; the elimination of distortions in competition within the common market;

> the creation of a Social Fund to improve job opportunities for workers and raise their standard of living;

> the adoption of common agricultural and transport policies; and

> the association of overseas developing countries with the Community in order to increase trade and promote economic and social development.

These objectives have been confirmed and augmented by the Single European Act of 1986 and the 1991 Maastricht Treaty on European Union.

European Union

The Rome Treaty's signatories declared themselves 'determined to establish the foundations of an ever closer union between the peoples of Europe'. This aim was restated in the Maastricht Treaty.

The nature of European union has never been formally defined. Successive British governments have opposed the creation of a unitary state or federal structure in which national sovereignty would be submerged. In practice, European union has been a step-by-step process of greater co-operation, building on existing policies and elaborating new ones within the framework of the Treaties.

Maastricht Treaty

The Maastricht Treaty amends the Rome Treaty and makes other commitments. It:

> introduces the concept of Union citizenship as a supplement to national citizenship, provides some measure of institutional reform and strengthens control of the Community's finances;

> provides on an intergovernmental basis for a common foreign and security policy and for greater co-operation on issues concerned with justice and home affairs;

> clarifies and codifies Community competences in areas such as regional strategy, consumer protection, education and vocational training, the environment and public health;

> provides for moves towards economic and monetary union; and

> embodies the principle of subsidiarity under which action is taken at Community level only if its objectives cannot be achieved by member states acting alone.

The 1992 Edinburgh summit agreed to apply a subsidiarity test to all future proposals for Community action. A review of existing EC legislation is under way to ensure that it conforms to the subsidiarity principle.

Following approval by Parliament, the Treaty was ratified by Britain in August 1993. All the other member states have also ratified the Treaty.

Economic and Monetary Union

During the negotiations on economic and monetary union (EMU), the Government sought to ensure that:

> there would be no commitment by Britain to move to a single monetary policy or single currency;

> monetary matters would remain a national responsibility until the Community moved to a single currency and monetary policy;

> member states would retain primary responsibility for their economic policies; and

> there were clear and quantifiable convergence conditions which member states would have to satisfy before moving to a single currency.

The Treaty provides for progress towards EMU in three stages: the first - completion of the single market - has been achieved. Under stage 2, a European Monetary Institute will be established with a largely advisory and consultative role. Although the Institute will prepare for stage 3, monetary policy will still be a national responsibility. Member states will co-ordinate economic policies in the context of agreed non-binding policy guidelines. The British Government supports the first and second stages of EMU.

Under the Treaty a single currency is envisaged by 1 January 1999, although member states will have to satisfy certain criteria on inflation rates, government deficit levels, currency fluctuation margins and interest rates. A special protocol recognises that Britain is not obliged or committed to move to this final stage of EMU without a separate decision to do so by the Government and Parliament at the appropriate time.

Key Data 94, © Crown copyright 1994

The Community Budget

The Community's revenue consists of:

> levies on agricultural imports;

> customs duties;

> the proceeds of a notional rate of value added tax (VAT) of up to 1.4 per cent on a standard 'basket' of goods and services; and

> contributions from member states based on gross national product (GNP).

> Overall Community revenue is limited by a ceiling of 1.2 per cent of Community GNP.

When it first joined the Community, Britain made a net contribution to the budget far in excess of that justified by its share of GNP. Following a series of negotiations to put this right, Britain has received since 1984 a rebate which is worth some £2,000 million a year.

An agreement on future Community finance was reached at the 1992 Edinburgh summit. Under this there is no increase in the revenue ceiling until 1995, when it will rise in steps, reaching 1.27 per cent of Community GNP in 1999. The revenue system will be reformed to ensure that member states' contributions reflect more accurately their relative prosperity. Agricultural spending will be less than half the Community budget by the end of the century, compared with 80 per cent in 1973 and 50 per cent at present. More resources will be allocated to the poorer regions of the Community.

Single Market

The Single European Act set the deadline of 31 December 1992 for the completion of the single market. The Edinburgh summit agreed that this programme had been successfully completed in all essential respects. The Government believes that the single market will reduce business costs, stimulate efficiency and encourage the creation of jobs and wealth. The single market programme covers, among other things, the liberalisation of capital movements, the opening up of public procurement markets and the mutual recognition of professional qualifications.

Transport

Britain fully supports the liberalisation of transport in the Community. Measures so far taken include the removal of permits and quotas on road haulage and the establishment of a single market in civil aviation. Airlines meeting established safety and common financial fitness criteria are entitled to an operating licence allowing virtually unrestricted access to routes within the Community. They are free to set fares and rates according to their commercial judgment.

In 1992 a regulation was agreed on slot allocation at airports designed to back up the single market in aviation; it aims to protect the legitimate interests of established carriers while promoting competition by assisting new entrants.

The opening of the Channel Tunnel in 1994 will improve Britain's links with other member states.

European Economic Area

In 1992 the Community reached an agreement with the seven members of the European Free Trade Association (EFTA) to extend free movement of goods, services and capital to the EFTA countries in a new European Economic Area (EEA). Implementation of this agreement was delayed by the result of a referendum in Switzerland which narrowly turned down Swiss membership of the EEA. The EEA is expected to be the world's largest single market when it comes into operation.

Trade

Britain is the world's fifth largest trading nation and the Community is the world's largest trading bloc, accounting for about a third of all trade.

The British Government fully supports a world open trading system on which EC member states depend for future economic growth and jobs.

Under the Rome Treaty, the European Commission speaks on behalf of Britain and the other EC member states in international trade negotiations, such as the various rounds of the General Agreement on Tariffs and Trade (GATT). The Commission negotiates on a mandate agreed by the Council of Ministers.

The Environment

The Community is at the forefront of many international measures on environmental issues, such as car exhaust pollution and the depletion of the ozone layer.

Agriculture and Fisheries

The Common Agricultural Policy (CAP) is designed to secure food supplies and to stabilise markets. It has also, however, created overproduction and unwanted food surpluses, placing a burden on the Community budget.

The Common Fisheries Policy is concerned with the rational conservation and management of fishery resources.

Structural Funds

The EC Structural Funds are designed to:

> promote economic development in poorer regions;

> improve regions seriously affected by industrial decline;

> combat long-term unemployment;

> train young people to find jobs; and

> promote development in rural areas.

Infrastructure projects and productive investments are financed by the European Regional Development Fund. The European Social Fund supports training and employment measures for the long-term unemployed and young people. The Guidance Section of the European Agricultural Guidance and Guarantee Fund supports agricultural restructuring and some rural development measures. A new fund to support restructuring in the fishing industry was created in 1993.

EUROPEAN COMMUNITY

Other Community programmes aim to assist the development of new economic activities in regions affected by the restructuring of traditional industries such as steel, coal and shipbuilding.

The European Investment Bank, a non-profit-making institution, lends at competitive interest rates to public and private capital projects. Lending is directed towards:

less-favoured regions;

transport infrastructure;

protection of the environment;

improving industrial competitiveness; and

supporting loans to small and medium-sized enterprises.

The Bank also provides loans in support of the Community's policy of co-operation with the countries of the Mediterranean basin, Central and Eastern Europe and the African, Caribbean and Pacific (ACP) states.

The Maastricht Treaty provides for the setting up of a Cohesion Fund in order to reduce the gaps between the prosperity of the poorest member states of the Community and the others. The Fund will finance projects on environmental protection and transport infrastructure in Spain, Portugal, Greece and the Irish Republic.

Employment and Social Affairs

In Britain's view, Community social policy should be primarily concerned with job creation and with maintaining a well-educated and trained workforce to ensure competitiveness in world markets. The Government supports:

measures to safeguard health and safety at work, freedom of movement for workers, Community-wide recognition of professional and vocational qualifications and equal opportunities at work; and

practical measures to increase jobs and cut unemployment.

The Government is opposed to measures which, in its view, would impose further regulations and costs on employers and damage Community competitiveness. For this reason, the Government negotiated a clause in the Maastricht Treaty, under which new and far-reaching Community powers in the social area apply only to the other 11 member states and not to Britain.

Research and Development

Community research collaboration is promoted primarily through a series of framework programmes defining priorities and setting out the overall level of funding. The British Government actively encourages British companies and organisations to participate in collaborative research and development (R&D) with European partners.

Under the current programme, which ends in 1994, priority is given to information technology (ESPRIT), telecommunications (RACE) and industrial materials and technologies; however, there are other important programmes covering the environment, biotechnology, agriculture, health and energy. There is also a scheme for the exchange of researchers.

Extract from BRITAIN 1994. Reproduced by kind permission of the Central Office of Information.

Key Data 94, © Crown copyright 1994

7.1   European Community Regions

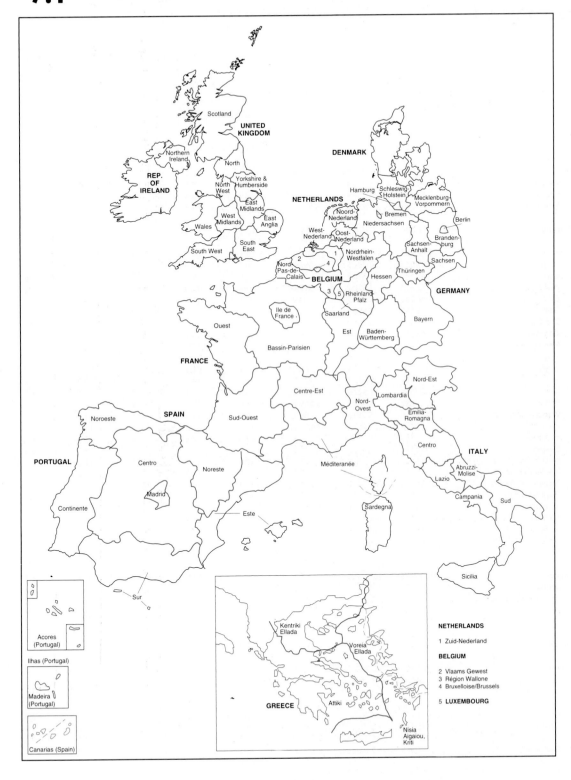

From: Regional Trends 1994

7.2 European Communities Comparisons

	Area (sq Km) 1991	Population[1] (thousands) 1991	Persons per sq km 1991	Percentage of population		Births (per 1 000 pop.) 1991	Deaths (per 1 000 pop.) 1991	Infant mortality (per 1 000 births) 1990
				Aged under 15 1991	Aged 65 or over 1991			
EUR 12	2 361 019	344 843.3	146.1	18.2	14.6	11.6	10.1	..
Belgium	30 518	10 004.5	327.8	18.1	15.0	12.5	10.4	..
Vlaams Gewest	13 512	5 781.4	427.9	18.0	14.5	12.2	9.7	..
Region Wallonne	16 844	3 267.4	194.0	18.7	15.3	12.9	11.3	..
Bruxelles-Brussels	161	955.8	5,921.8	17.4	17.4	13.4	11.8	..
Denmark	43 080	5 154.0	119.6	17.0	15.6	12.5	11.6	..
France	543 965	57 055.4	104.9	20.1	14.1	13.3	9.1	7.3
Ile de France	12 012	10 781.5	897.5	20.3	10.9	15.7	7.3	7.2
Bassin Parisien	145 645	10 320.8	70.9	20.9	14.3	13.1	9.4	7.8
Nord-Pas-de-Calais	12 414	3 970.2	319.8	23.4	12.0	14.8	9.3	8.2
Est	48 030	5 039.7	104.9	20.6	12.7	13.5	8.8	7.2
Ouest	85 099	7 496.5	88.1	20.2	15.4	12.1	9.6	7.0
Sud-Ouest	103 599	5 987.2	57.8	17.3	17.8	10.8	10.7	7.5
Centre-Est	69 711	6 735.5	96.6	20.0	13.8	13.1	8.9	6.6
Mediterranee	67 455	6 724.0	99.7	18.4	17.1	12.3	10.3	6.9
Germany[2]	356 854	80 013.9	224.2	16.2	14.9	10.4	11.4	..
Baden-Württemberg	35 751	9 911.9	277.2	16.1	14.3	11.9	9.8	6.5
Bayern	70 554	11 522.4	163.3	15.8	15.1	11.7	10.6	6.3
Berlin	889	3 439.9	3 869.0	16.0	14.1	8.9	12.7	6.6
Brandenburg	29 056	2 560.5	88.1	20.5	12.1	6.7	12.2	..
Bremen	404	682.7	1 688.8	13.2	17.5	10.0	12.6	7.5
Hamburg	755	1 660.6	2 198.5	12.7	17.6	9.9	12.9	6.2
Hessen	21 114	5 800.3	274.7	14.8	15.5	10.6	11.0	6.3
Mecklenburg-Vorpommern	23 559	1 907.8	81.0	22.0	10.9	7.1	11.3	..
Niedersachsen	47 349	7 431.5	157.0	15.4	15.8	11.2	11.5	6.9
Nordrhein-Westfalen	34 068	17 429.8	511.6	15.4	15.1	11.4	11.1	3.2
Rheinland-Pfalz	19 849	3 792.4	191.1	15.7	15.9	11.2	11.5	8.2
Saarland	2 570	1 074.9	418.2	14.7	15.6	10.3	11.8	6.7
Sachsen	18 341	4 721.6	257.4	18.5	15.7	6.6	14.0	..
Sachsen-Anhalt	20 607	2 848.6	138.2	18.9	14.1	6.8	13.4	..
Schleswig-Holstein	15 731	2 637.3	167.7	14.8	16.0	11.0	11.8	6.8
Thüringen	16 251	2 591.7	159.5	19.6	13.7	6.8	12.3	..
Greece	131 957	10 200.0	77.3	18.7	14.2	10.1	9.4	9.7
Voreia Ellada	56 792	3 321.1	58.5	18.6	12.3	9.9	9.1	9.7
Kentriki Ellada	53 899	2 420.8	44.9	18.0	17.6	9.1	10.3	8.9
Attiki	3 808	3 466.7	910.4	18.9	12.6	10.6	8.7	10.8
Nisia Aigaiou, Kriti	17 458	991.3	56.8	20.3	17.4	11.0	10.0	7.5
Ireland	68 895	3 523.8	51.1	26.9	11.4	15.0	8.9	..
Italy	301 287	56 760.0	188.4	16.5	15.1	9.8	9.6	8.2
Nord Ovest	34 079	6 103.3	179.1	12.5	18.4	7.4	11.8	6.8
Lombardia	23 859	8 855.2	371.2	14.3	14.6	8.5	9.5	7.0
Nord Est	39 827	6 463.7	162.3	14.5	15.5	8.7	9.8	5.6
Emilia-Romagna	22 123	3 907.3	176.6	11.8	19.0	7.1	11.4	6.9
Centro	41 142	5 771.1	140.3	13.3	18.6	7.6	11.1	7.0
Lazio	17 203	5 135.7	298.5	15.9	13.9	9.6	8.8	7.1
Campania	13 595	5 624.7	413.7	23.0	11.3	14.1	7.9	10.4
Abruzzi-Molise	15 232	1 578.9	103.7	17.2	16.3	9.9	10.0	8.2
Sud	44 430	6 707.9	151.0	21.3	12.6	12.4	8.0	9.7
Sicilia	25 707	4 965.8	193.2	21.6	13.6	13.0	9.1	10.6
Sardegna	24 090	1 646.3	68.3	18.8	12.2	9.9	8.1	9.3

7.7 Purchasing power of the pound in the European Community[1], 1981 and 1992

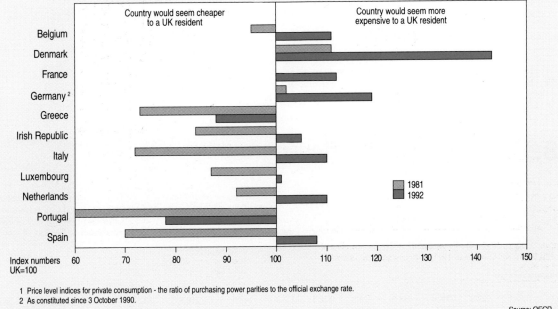

Country would seem cheaper to a UK resident

Country would seem more expensive to a UK resident

1981
1992

Index numbers UK=100

1 Price level indices for private consumption - the ratio of purchasing power parities to the official exchange rate.
2 As constituted since 3 October 1990.

Source: OECD

From: Social Trends 1994, Chart 6.11

Definitions and sources

The General Index of Retail Prices (RPI) measures the changes month by month in the level of prices of the goods and services purchased by all types of household in the UK, with the exception of some higher income households and retired people mainly dependent on state benefits. A special pensioner price index is published in *Economic Trends* and in the *Department of Employment Gazette*.

The Tax and Price Index (TPI) is described in a footnote to the table in which it appears.

The Producer Price Index has replaced what was called the Wholesale Price Index. The new title is more accurate and conforms with international nomenclatures. The index was also re-based from 1975 to 1980. Full details were given in an article in *British Business*, 15 April 1983.

For other sources see:

Guide to Official Statistics, 1990 edition (200 pages approximately, fully indexed) HMSO.

8.1 General index of retail prices[1]

	All items	All items except seasonal food[2]	Food	Alcoholic drink	Tobacco	Housing	Fuel and light	Durable household goods	Clothing and footwear	Transport and vehicles	Miscellan-eous goods	Services	Meals bought and consumed outside the home
15 January 1974 = 100													
Annual averages													
1982	320.4	322.0	299.3	341.0	413.3	358.3	433.3	243.8	210.5	343.5	325.8	331.6	341.7
1983	335.1	337.1	308.8	366.4	440.9	367.1	465.4	250.4	214.8	366.3	345.6	342.9	364.0
1984	351.8	353.1	326.1	387.7	489.0	400.7	478.8	256.7	214.6	374.7	364.7	357.3	390.8
1985	373.2	375.4	336.3	412.1	532.4	452.3	499.3	263.9	222.9	392.5	392.2	381.3	413.3
1986	385.9	387.9	347.3	430.6	584.9	478.1	506.0	266.7	229.2	390.1	409.2	400.5	439.5
1987 Jan	394.5	396.4	354.0	440.7	602.9	502.4	506.1	265.6	230.8	399.7	413.0	408.8	454.8

continued overleaf

8.1 General index of retail prices[1]
continued

	All items	All items excluding				Food				Alcohol and tobacco	Housing and household expend-iture	Personal expend-iture	Travel and leisure	Consumer durables
		Food	Seasonal food[2]	Housing	Mortgage interest payments	All	Seasonal food[2]	Non-seasonal food	Food and catering					
Weights														
1993	1 000	856	979	836	952	144	21	123	189	113	336	97	265	127
1994	..	..	..	..	..	142	..	..	..	..	..	..	..	..
13 January 1987=100														
Annual averages														
1989	115.2	116.1	115.5	111.5	112.9	110.5	105.0	111.6	111.9	110.8	121.9	111.3	112.8	107.2
1990	126.1	127.4	126.4	119.2	122.1	119.4	116.4	119.9	120.9	120.6	139.0	117.6	119.8	111.3
1991	133.5	135.1	133.8	128.3	130.3	125.6	121.6	126.3	128.6	136.2	142.2	123.6	128.9	114.8
1992	138.5	140.5	139.1	134.3	136.4	128.3	114.7	130.6	132.6	146.8	144.2	126.9	136.8	115.5
1993	140.7	142.6	141.4	138.4	140.5	130.6	111.4	134.0	136.1	155.1	141.2	129.5	141.8	115.9
Monthly figures														
1992														
Mar	136.7	138.2	137.0	133.0	134.5	129.4	124.8	130.2	133.0	142.7	141.9	126.1	134.6	115.7
Apr	138.8	140.7	139.2	134.4	136.7	128.9	122.4	130.1	132.8	146.6	144.8	127.3	136.9	116.2
May	139.3	141.2	139.7	134.9	137.1	129.5	120.9	131.0	133.4	147.3	145.1	127.5	137.5	116.4
Jun	139.3	141.3	139.9	135.0	137.2	129.0	117.4	131.0	133.1	147.6	145.0	127.7	137.8	116.4
Jul	138.8	141.1	139.6	134.3	136.7	127.2	105.8	130.9	131.9	148.1	145.0	125.0	137.8	113.1
Aug	138.9	141.2	139.7	134.4	136.9	127.5	107.0	131.1	132.2	148.4	145.2	125.0	137.7	113.5
Sep	139.4	141.8	140.3	134.9	137.3	127.1	104.0	131.1	132.0	148.7	145.6	128.2	137.7	116.0
Oct	139.9	142.3	140.7	135.5	137.8	127.4	106.5	131.1	132.4	149.2	145.8	129.3	138.3	116.8
Nov	139.7	142.1	140.5	135.6	137.9	127.3	106.3	130.9	132.4	149.5	145.1	129.2	138.4	116.8
Dec	139.2	141.3	139.9	135.7	138.1	128.4	110.6	131.5	133.4	149.8	143.4	128.7	138.0	117.1
1993														
Jan	137.9	139.7	138.6	135.0	137.4	128.8	112.2	131.7	133.8	150.6	140.7	125.2	137.2	112.8
Feb	138.8	140.5	139.4	136.0	138.3	130.2	114.6	132.9	135.0	151.1	141.2	126.9	138.2	114.5
Mar	139.3	140.8	139.8	137.0	139.2	131.3	116.3	133.9	136.1	151.6	140.5	128.6	139.0	115.9
Apr	140.6	142.5	141.3	138.4	140.6	130.8	113.0	134.0	136.0	154.7	141.1	130.1	141.6	117.0
May	141.1	142.8	141.6	139.0	141.0	132.2	118.0	134.6	137.2	155.3	141.0	130.5	142.1	117.3
Jun	141.0	142.9	141.7	138.9	141.0	131.4	112.6	134.7	136.8	155.5	140.7	129.6	143.0	116.3
Jul	140.7	142.6	141.5	138.5	140.6	131.3	109.4	135.3	136.8	156.0	140.5	127.0	142.9	113.3
Aug	141.3	143.2	142.1	139.1	141.2	131.5	110.8	135.2	137.0	156.8	141.1	128.5	143.3	114.8
Sep	141.9	144.1	142.8	139.8	141.8	130.9	108.3	135.0	136.7	157.4	141.5	131.5	143.9	117.0
Oct	141.8	144.1	142.7	139.6	141.7	130.0	106.2	134.3	136.1	157.7	141.6	131.9	143.6	116.9
Nov	141.6	144.0	142.5	139.3	141.4	129.1	105.7	133.4	135.5	157.2	141.9	132.4	142.8	117.4
Dec	141.9	144.3	142.8	139.7	141.8	129.4	109.7	133.0	135.8	157.8	142.0	132.0	143.6	117.6
1994														
Jan	141.3	143.5	142.1	139.3	141.3	130.0	110.3	133.5	136.3	159.8	140.3	127.8	144.0	113.0
Feb	142.1	144.3	142.9	140.2	142.2	130.8	112.6	134.0	137.0	160.3	140.6	131.0	144.6	114.8
Mar	142.5	144.7	143.2	140.6	142.6	131.6	115.1	134.4	137.8	160.2	140.9	131.5	145.1	116.2

1 Following the recommendation of the Retail Price Index Advisory Committee, the index has been re-referenced to make 13 January 1987=100. Further details can be found in the April 1987 edition of *Employment Gazette*.
2 Seasonal food is defined as: items of food the prices of which show significant seasonal variations. These are fresh fruit and vegetables, fresh fish, eggs and home-killed lamb.

Source: Central Statistical Office

From: Monthly Digest of Statistics, May 1994, Table 18.1

PRICES

8.2 Tax and Price Index

	January 1978=100							January 1987=100						
	1981	1982	1983	1984	1985	1 986	1987	1987	1988	1989	1990	1991	1992	1993	1994
January	140.4	162.3	170.7	177.9	184.7	192.9	198.0	100.0	101.4	107.1	113.9	123.6	128.1	128.7	132.1
February	141.9	162.4	171.6	178.8	186.4	193.7	..	100.5	101.8	108.0	114.7	124.3	128.8	129.6	132.9
March	144.3	164.0	171.9	179.4	188.4	194.0	..	100.7	102.3	108.5	115.9	124.9	129.3	130.2	133.4
April	151.3	166.0	171.8	178.8	190.2	192.5	..	99.7	101.4	109.8	118.2	125.4	129.6	131.3	..
May	152.4	167.4	172.6	179.6	191.2	192.9	..	99.8	101.9	110.5	119.4	125.8	130.2	131.8	..
June	153.5	168.0	173.1	180.1	191.7	192.8	..	99.8	102.3	110.9	119.9	126.5	130.2	131.7	..
July	154.2	169.0	174.2	179.9	191.3	192.1	..	99.7	102.4	111.1	120.0	126.2	129.6	131.4	..
August	155.5	169.0	175.1	181.8	191.8	192.9	..	100.0	103.7	111.4	121.4	126.5	129.7	132.1	..
September	156.6	168.9	176.0	182.2	191.7	194.0	..	100.4	104.3	112.2	122.7	127.0	130.3	132.7	..
October	158.2	169.9	176.7	183.5	191.4	194.3	..	100.9	105.4	111.7	123.8	127.5	130.8	132.6	..
November	160.1	170.9	177.5	184.1	192.1	196.3	..	101.5	106.0	112.8	123.4	128.1	130.6	132.4	..
December	161.2	170.5	178.0	183.9	192.4	197.1	..	101.4	106.3	113.1	123.3	128.2	130.1	132.7	..

Percentage changes on one year earlier

Tax and price index

	1981	1982	1983	1984	1985	1 986	1987	1987	1988	1989	1990	1991	1992	1993	1994
January	14.0	15.6	5.2	4.2	3.8	4.4	2.6		1.4	5.6	6.3	8.5	3.6	0.5	2.6
February	13.2	14.4	5.7	4.2	4.3	3.9	..	2.7	1.3	6.1	6.2	8.4	3.6	0.6	2.5
March	13.4	13.7	4.8	4.4	5.0	3.0	..	2.8	1.6	6.1	6.8	7.8	3.5	0.7	2.5
April	15.7	9.7	3.5	4.1	6.4	1.2	..	2.5	1.7	8.3	7.7	6.1	3.3	1.3	..
May	15.3	9.8	3.1	4.1	6.5	0.9	..	2.4	2.1	8.4	8.1	5.4	3.5	1.2	..
June	14.9	9.4	3.0	4.0	6.4	0.6	..	2.5	2.5	8.4	8.1	5.5	2.9	1.2	..
July	14.3	9.6	3.1	3.3	6.3	0.4	..	2.8	2.7	8. 5	8.0	5.2	2.7	1.4	..
August	14.9	8.7	3.6	3.8	5.5	0.6	..	2.6	3.7	7. 4	9.0	4.2	2.5	1.9	..
September	14.9	7.9	4.2	3.5	5.2	1.2	..	2.4	3.9	7. 6	9.4	3.5	2.6	1.8	..
October	15.2	7.4	4.0	3.8	4.3	1.5	..	2.9	4.5	6. 0	10.8	3.0	26	1.4	..
November	15.6	6.7	3.9	3.7	4.3	2.2	..	2.4	4.4	6. 4	9.4	3.8	2.0	1.4	..
December	15.6	5.8	4.4	3.3	4.6	2.4	..	1.9	4.8	6. 4	9.0	4.0	1.5	2.0	..

Retail prices index

	1981	1982	1983	1984	1985	1 986	1987	1987	1988	1989	1990	1991	1992	1993	1994
January	13.0	12.0	4.9	5.1	5.0	5.5	3.9		3.3	7.5	7.7	9.0	4.1	1.7	2.5
February	12.5	11.0	5.3	5.1	5.4	5.1	..	3.9	3.3	7.8	7.5	8.9	4.1	1.8	2.4
March	12.6	10.4	4.6	5.2	6.1	4.2	..	4.0	3.5	7.9	8.1	8.2	4.0	1.9	2.3
April	12.0	9.4	4.0	5.2	6.9	3.0	..	4.2	3.9	8.0	9.4	6.4	4.3	1.3	..
May	11.7	9.5	3.7	5.1	7.0	2.8	..	4.1	4.2	8.3	9.7	5.8	4.3	1.3	..
June	11.3	9.2	3.7	5.1	7.0	2.5	..	4.2	4.6	8.3	9.8	5.8	3.9	1.2	..
July	10.9	8.7	4.2	4.5	6.9	2.4	..	4.4	4.8	8.2	9.8	5.5	3.7	1.4	..
August	11.5	8.0	4.6	5.0	6.2	2.4	..	4.4	5.7	7.3	10.6	4.7	3.6	1.7	..
September	11.4	7.3	5.1	4.7	5.9	3.0	..	4.2	5.9	7.6	10.9	4.1	3.6	1.8	..
October	11.7	6.8	5.0	5.0	5.4	3.0	..	4.5	6.4	7.3	10.9	3.7	3.6	1.4	..
November	12.0	6.3	4.8	4.9	5.5	3.5	..	4.1	6.4	7.7	9.7	4.3	3.0	1.4	..
December	12.0	5.4	5.3	4.6	5.7	3.7	..	3.7	6.8	7.7	9.3	4.5	2.6	1.9	..

Note: The purpose and methodology of the Tax and Price Index were described in an article in the August 1979 issue of *Economic Trends* and in the September *Economic Progress Report* published by the Treasury. The purpose is to produce a single index which measures changes in both direct taxes (including national insurance contributions) and in retail prices for a representative cross-section of taxpayers. Thus, while the Retail Prices Index may be used to measure changes in the purchasing power of after-tax income (and of the income of non-taxpayers) the Tax and Price Index takes account of the fact that taxpayers will have more or less to spend according to changes in direct taxation. The Index measures the change in gross taxable income which would maintain after-tax income in real terms.

Source: Central Statistical Office

From: Monthly Digest of Statistics, May 1994, Table 18.5

Key Data 94, © Crown copyright 1994

8.3 Purchasing power of a 1951 pound

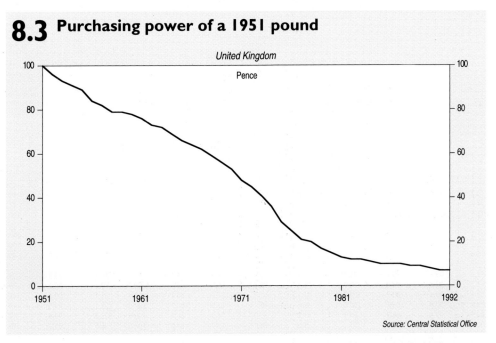

United Kingdom

Pence

Source: Central Statistical Office

From: Social Trends 1994, Chart 6.1

8.4 Consumer credit : amount outstanding

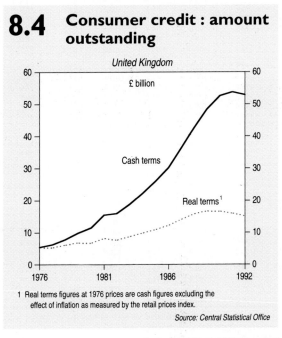

United Kingdom

£ billion

Cash terms

Real terms[1]

1 Real terms figures at 1976 prices are cash figures excluding the effect of inflation as measured by the retail prices index.

Source: Central Statistical Office

From: Social Trends 1994, Chart 6.14

PRICES

8.5   Index numbers of producer prices

1990=100, monthly averages

| | | | | Material and fuel purchased[1,2] | | | | | | | | |
	Manufac- turing industry	Materials	Fuel	Manufac- turing other than food, drink and tobacco	Food, drink and tobacco manufac- turing indus- tries	Metal manufac- turing	Extrac- tion of minerals not elsewhere specified	Non- metallic mineral products	Chemical industry	Man- made fibres	Metal goods, engine- ring and vehicle indus- tries	Metal goods not elsewhere specified	Mechan- ical engin- eering
SIC 1980 Division Class or Group	2 to 4		2 to 4	2 to 4 excl 4 1/42	41/42	22	23	24	25	26	3	31	32
1989	100.8	102.2	95.2	100.7	100.1	104.3	94.9	96.1	95.8	97.8	101.7	103.2	99.1
1990	99.9	100.0	100.0	100.0	100.0	100.0	100.0	1 00.0	100.0	100.0	99.9	100.0	100.0
1991	98.2	97.5	100.9	97.4	101.0	96.0	102.8	1 02.8	100.5	100.3	99.4	98.0	102.0
1992	97.7	96.7	101.7	95.4	103.5	93.4	104.6	1 03.8	99.0	100.0	99.4	97.2	103.2
1993	102.2	101.6	105.1	99.0	109.2	95.8	108.2	1 06.0	103.4	104.4	103.5	100.9	107.5
1990 Apr	101.2	103.1	93.7	99.7	103.8	102.4	96.6	99.0	97.1	99.0	100.1	100.7	100.1
May	100.1	102.2	91.7	98.9	102.6	101.5	96.1	98.3	96.4	98.9	99.7	100.5	99.6
Jun	98.8	100.9	90.2	97.6	101.4	100.0	95.3	98.2	95.1	98.6	98.8	99.6	99.1
Jul	97.4	99.1	90.7	96.7	99.2	98.3	95.3	9 8.2	94.9	98.3	98.7	99.1	99.2
Aug	97.3	97.6	96.0	98.0	96.6	98.3	98.7	9 9.0	98.7	98.2	99.1	99.4	99.5
Sep	99.4	99.1	100.7	100.8	97.1	102.9	100.6	1 00.2	103.4	99.1	100.1	100.5	100.0
Oct	99.0	97.4	105.7	100.6	96.6	98.5	102.8	1 01.3	107.0	102.1	99.5	99.4	100.1
Nov	98.9	97.0	106.9	99.8	97.9	95.0	104.3	1 01.9	105.9	103.2	99.4	98.5	100.2
Dec	100.6	97.5	113.3	101.2	99.8	96.5	107.7	1 04.0	104.9	104.5	101.0	99.5	101.4
1991 Jan	100.0	97.2	111.7	100.3	100.4	95.9	108.3	1 04.6	104.0	103.6	101.0	99.1	102.0
Feb	98.8	97.2	105.7	98.2	101.1	94.1	105.1	1 03.4	101.9	101.7	100.0	98.6	101.5
Mar	98.4	98.8	96.7	96.8	102.7	95.6	100.3	1 01.7	99.4	101.1	99.5	98.6	101.4
Apr	99.5	99.6	99.0	98.0	103.6	98.0	101.5	1 02.4	100.0	100.9	100.4	99.3	102.5
May	99.1	99.4	98.3	97.5	103.5	97.2	101.3	1 02.2	100.6	100.3	99.8	98.8	102.2
Jun	98.5	99.2	95.9	97.3	102.1	97.9	100.7	1 01.7	99.8	100.1	99.4	98.2	102.2
Jul	97.4	97.6	96.8	97.3	99.2	97.8	100.8	1 02.4	100.1	99.4	99.3	98.0	102.2
Aug	96.2	96.1	96.8	96.5	97.5	96.4	100.8	1 02.4	99.8	99.2	98.8	97.6	101.9
Sep	96.3	96.2	96.9	96.1	98.4	95.2	101.4	1 02.2	99.4	98.9	98.4	97.0	101.5
Oct	96.8	96.2	99.4	96.4	99.3	95.9	101.9	1 02.4	100.3	99.2	98.3	96.7	101.7
Nov	97.9	96.5	104.0	96.9	101.4	94.4	104.4	1 03.1	100.6	99.3	98.8	96.7	102.1
Dec	99.0	96.4	109.9	97.7	102.8	93.5	106.5	1 04.5	100.0	100.0	99.7	97.1	102.8
1992 Jan	98.2	95.7	108.5	96.3	103.2	93.3	105.8	1 04.8	98.6	100.2	99.5	96.5	103.0
Feb	98.3	96.9	103.9	95.7	104.5	94.4	103.6	1 03.9	98.0	99.7	99.3	97.0	102.9
Mar	97.2	97.6	95.9	94.4	104.4	95.1	100.9	1 02.4	97.2	99.0	98.6	96.8	102.5
Apr	97.7	97.4	99.3	94.8	104.8	94.4	103.1	1 03.2	97.6	99.3	99.1	97.3	103.0
May	97.2	96.5	100.1	94.5	104.1	92.4	103.4	1 03.4	98.0	99.0	99.0	97.0	103.1
Jun	95.8	95.7	96.3	93.1	102.8	90.0	103.0	1 02.2	97.5	98.5	98.3	96.3	102.5
Jul	95.2	94.7	97.6	92.9	101.5	90.0	103.2	1 02.5	96.9	98.4	98.5	96.5	102.6
Aug	94.4	93.9	96.5	92.3	100.4	89.5	103.0	1 02.3	96.1	98.4	98.4	96.2	102.5
Sep	95.4	94.7	98.2	93.6	100.7	91.2	103.5	1 03.0	97.6	99.3	98.8	96.5	102.9
Oct	98.0	97.4	100.6	96.2	102.9	94.3	105.4	1 03.9	100.9	100.7	99.8	97.7	103.7
Nov	101.5	99.9	107.9	99.8	105.3	97.8	108.9	1 05.9	104.4	103.1	101.0	98.5	104.3
Dec	103.3	100.4	115.3	101.5	107.1	99.0	111.5	1 07.8	104.6	104.2	102.7	99.5	105.5
1993 Jan	103.9	101.7	113.0	101.2	109.2	98.9	110.7	1 07.1	104.6	105.1	102.9	99.8	106.1
Feb	104.4	103.5	108.2	101.1	110.8	100.8	108.5	1 05.9	105.3	105.6	103.0	100.3	106.4
Mar	104.6	104.4	105.3	100.1	113.2	99.5	108.1	1 05.4	104.9	104.7	102.7	100.2	106.3
Apr	103.9	103.8	104.3	98.8	113.8	96.3	108.4	1 05.9	104.0	105.3	102.7	100.1	106.6
May	103.2	103.3	103.0	97.9	113.7	93.4	108.2	1 05.7	103.4	104.6	102.4	99.7	106.5
Jun	102.9	103.0	102.4	98.2	112.4	94.5	107.5	1 05.6	103.0	104.3	102.8	100.4	106.9
Jul	101.7	101.7	102.0	98.2	109.3	95.6	106.9	1 05.5	102.2	102.9	104.0	101.7	108.1
Aug	100.8	100.7	101.0	98.0	106.9	95.5	106.6	1 05.2	102.3	103.7	104.1	101.8	107.9
Sep	99.5	99.1	101.1	97.2	105.0	93.2	106.3	1 05.2	102.2	103.8	103.6	101.3	108.1
Oct	98.9	98.3	102.5	97.5	103.6	92.5	106.8	1 05.7	102.6	103.8	103.6	101.0	108.3
Nov	100.8	99.2	107.8	99.1	105.0	94.1	109.3	1 06.9	103.4	104.6	104.7	101.7	108.9
Dec	102.2	100.1	111.1	100.2	107.0	95.4	110.9	1 07.9	103.2	104.6	105.6	102.5	109.4
1994 Jan	101.4	99.7	108.4	99.8	105.5	95.8	110.4	107.8	102.2	103.5	106.9	103.9	110.8
Feb	102.3	101.3	107.0	100.2	107.4	97.4	110.3	107.8	102.3	103.9p†	107.0	104.4	110.9
Mar	102.5p†	102.9p†	101.3p†	99.0p†	110.2p	97.0p	108.4p	107.0p	101.3p†	103.2p†	106.5p	104.4p†	110.7p†
Apr	102.7p	103.4p	100.3p	99.2 p	110.4p	96.9p	108.0p	107.0p	101.8p	103.4p	106.5p	104.5p	110.9p

Note: The dagger symbol beside a figure indicates the earliest revised value for each series. Figures marked with a 'p' are provisional.
1 Index numbers are constructed on a net sector basis ie transactions within sector are excluded.
2 Index numbers are compiled exclusive of VAT. Revenue duties (on cigarettes, tobacco and alcoholic liquor) are included, as is duty on hydrocarbon oils.

Source: Central Statistical Office

From: Monthly Digest of Statistics, May 1994, Table 18.6
Key Data 94, © Crown copyright 1994

8.5 Index numbers of producer prices
continued

1990=100 monthly averages

Price index numbers of materials and fuel purchased[1,2]

	Electrical and electronic engineering	Motor vehicles and parts	Other transport equipment	Instrument engineering	Food manufacturing industries	Materials	Fuel	Textile industry	Footwear and clothing Industries	Timber and wooden furniture industries	Paper and paper products	Processing of rubber and plastics	Other manufacturing industries	Construction materials	House-building materials
SIC 1980 Division Class or Group	34	35	36	37	411 to 423			43	45	46	47	48	49	5	part of 5
1989	99.4	96.7	96.6	95.3	100.3	100.4	96.9	101.7	9 7.3	92.7	97.4	99.4	100.9	94.0	94.2
1990	99.9	100.0	100.0	100.0	100.0	100.0	100.0	100.0	100.0	100.0	100.0	100.0	100.0	100.0	100.0
1991	100.4	103.2	102.9	103.9	101.0	100.9	102.1	96.0	101.2	100.8	98.1	97.5	98.1	103.9	102.9
1992	101.0	105.4	104.7	105.2	103.6	103.5	105.0	94.4	102.1	100.3	95.3	95.4	96.3	104.7	103.0
1993	104.3	109.1	107.0	107.9	109.4	109.4	108.7	94.8	104.5	106.3	93.5	98.9	102.2	108.1	106.4
1990 Apr	100.3	99.5	99.4	99.5	104.1	104.5	94.0	102.4	100.9	99.3	99.7	98.4	101.5	99.7	99.8
May	100.0	99.5	99.3	99.3	102.9	103.3	92.2	100.9	100.3	99.6	100.0	98.5	100.8	99.8	100.0
Jun	99.3	99.4	99.1	99.3	101.5	102.0	90.7	100.2	100.1	100.1	99.8	98.1	99.4	100.0	100.1
Jul	99.4	99.7	99.1	99.5	99.1	99.5	91.5	98.3	99.6	100.3	99.7	98.1	99.7	100.4	100.6
Aug	99.8	100.2	99.9	100.1	96.3	96.4	95.5	97.2	99.1	100.7	99.6	98.2	99.8	100.8	101.2
Sep	100.5	100.5	100.6	100.4	97.0	97.0	97.0	97.5	99.2	101.0	99.6	99.5	100.2	101.2	101.1
Oct	99.7	100.8	101.3	100.9	96.4	96.2	100.6	96.9	99.1	100.9	99.0	101.3	97.6	101.6	101.1
Nov	99.5	101.1	101.4	101.4	97.8	97.5	104.9	96.1	98.9	100.7	99.5	103.7	97.0	101.5	101.0
Dec	100.5	101.6	102.2	102.2	99.7	99.1	115.4	97.8	99.2	101.5	100.0	105.0	97.9	101.5	101.0
1991 Jan	101.3	102.6	103.1	103.6	100.2	99.6	114.4	98.2	99.5	102.0	99.3	105.1	98.5	102.8	102.2
Feb	100.4	102.5	103.0	103.5	101.1	100.8	106.7	96.4	99.2	101.6	99.4	103.3	96.6	102.7	102.2
Mar	100.3	102.6	102.4	103.5	102.8	103.0	96.9	95.8	100.7	100.9	98.2	101.1	98.4	104.4	103.6
Apr	101.1	103.2	103.0	104.2	103.7	103.8	100.9	96.2	101.4	100.1	98.8	98.4	99.8	104.4	103.4
May	100.6	103.2	103.0	104.1	103.6	103.8	99.1	96.4	101.5	100.4	98.1	96.3	99.2	104.4	103.4
Jun	100.4	103.0	102.6	104.0	102.0	102.3	96.5	96.1	102.3	100.6	97.9	95.7	100.3	104.0	103.0
Jul	100.5	103.1	102.8	104.4	99.0	99.1	97.4	95.8	102.2	100.6	97.8	95.3	100.2	104.2	103.3
Aug	100.0	103.4	102.8	103.5	97.2	97.2	97.1	95.5	101.9	100.4	97.6	95.1	97.9	104.1	103.1
Sep	99.8	103.5	102.7	103.5	98.3	98.3	97.4	95.1	101.6	100.7	97.4	95.5	97.0	104.1	103.0
Oct	99.9	103.5	102.8	103.7	99.2	99.2	99.3	94.2	101.5	100.7	96.6	94.9	97.4	104.2	103.1
Nov	100.1	103.7	103.0	104.0	101.4	101.2	105.7	95.3	101.4	100.5	97.3	94.6	96.4	104.0	102.6
Dec	100.3	104.1	103.7	104.4	102.9	102.4	114.2	96.6	101.7	100.8	98.7	95.2	95.3	104.0	102.4
1992 Jan	100.6	104.6	104.3	105.3	103.3	102.8	113.9	95.5	101.9	100.6	95.6	95.8	95.1	103.9	102.7
Feb	100.6	104.6	104.2	105.1	104.7	104.6	107.7	95.5	102.1	100.5	95.1	95.2	96.3	104.0	102.4
Mar	100.2	104.5	103.8	104.7	104.6	104.9	97.6	94.9	102.1	99.8	94.3	94.4	96.6	104.4	103.0
Apr	100.6	104.9	104.5	104.9	105.0	105.1	102.4	95.0	102.1	100.2	95.2	94.4	96.1	104.7	103.2
May	100.5	105.1	104.7	105.0	104.2	104.2	103.2	94.6	101.9	100.0	95.0	94.4	95.1	104.6	103.0
Jun	100.1	105.1	104.5	104.8	102.9	103.1	98.8	93.3	101.4	99.8	94.6	94.4	94.6	104.5	102.9
Jul	100.4	105.1	104.4	104.9	101.5	101.5	101.0	92.7	101.0	99.4	94.5	94.1	94.6	104.6	103.0
Aug	100.3	105 4	104.5	105.1	100.3	100.3	99.9	92.4	100.9	99.3	94.4	94.2	93.8	104.8	103.0
Sep	100.6	105.6	104.6	105.2	100.6	100.6	101.3	92.7	101.6	99.5	94.5	94.7	94.9	104.8	103.0
Oct	101.7	106.1	105.2	105.5	102.9	102.9	102.9	94.1	102.6	100.4	95.0	96.2	97.9	105.0	103.1
Nov	102.8	106.5	105.5	105.8	105.4	105.2	110.9	95.6	103.7	101.7	97.3	97.7	100.3	105.2	103.1
Dec	103.8	107.3	106.2	106.4	107.2	106.6	120.7	96.0	104.1	102.4	98.1	98.8	100.5	105.5	103.3
1993 Jan	104.3	107.9	106.7	107.4	109.4	109.1	117.9	96.4	104.5	103.5	96.4	98.9	100.9	106.0	103.7
Feb	104.5	108.2	106.7	107.3	111.1	111.1	111.1	96.2	104.8	104.3	94.4	98.9	102.8	106.3	104.3
Mar	104.0	108.4	106.7	107.4	113.6	113.8	107.3	95.4	104.5	104.6	94.0	98.6	101.7	106.8	104.7
Apr	103.6	108.6	106.9	107.4	114.1	114.3	107.1	94.5	104.0	104.8	93.8	98.9	100.2	107.4	105.4
May	103.4	108.6	106.2	107.1	114.0	114.4	106.0	94.2	104.0	104.6	93.4	99.1	101.0	107.8	106.2
Jun	103.9	108.9	106.4	107.4	113.1	113.4	105.1	94.4	104.1	106.0	93.4	99.1	102.2	108.3	106.7
Jul	104.8	109.3	107.0	108.4	109.6	109.8	105.3	94.5	104.2	106.5 -	92.9	98.6	104.4	108.8	107.2
Aug	104.8	109.6	107.1	108.2	107.0	107.1	104.4	94.0	104.2	107.0	92.8	98.1	103.7	109.0	107.4
Sep	104.0	109.7	107.0	108.0	105.1	105.2	103.9	93.7	104.1	107.1	92.5	97.9	100.9	109.2	107.5
Oct	103.9	109.9	107.3	108.2	103.6	103.6	105.7	94.0	104.4	108.8	92.6	98.6	101.5	109.2	107.7
Nov	104.8	110.1	107.8	108.7	105.1	104.8	112.6	95.2	105.2	108.5	93.0	99.8	103.0	109.1	107.6
Dec	105.7	110.3	108.1	109.0	107.1	106.6	118.5	95.7	105.7	109.5	93.3	100.2	103.9	109.4	107.9
1994 Jan	106.8	111.3	108.8 p†	109.5 p†	105.6	105.1	116.0†	95.4	106.1 †	110.3	93.2	99.6 †	104.5 †	110.4†	109.3 p†
Feb	107.1	111.4	108.9 p	109.4 p†	107.6	107.4	114.2	95.9†	106.7 †	111.1	93.2 p	99.2	105.1 p	110.8 p	109.9 p
Mar	106.8 p	111.4 p	108.9 p	109.5 p	110.5 p†	110.7 p	107.4 p	95.4 p	106.9 p	111.2 p	92.9 p	98.6 p	105.1 p†	111.6 p	110.7 p
Apr	106.9 p	111.6 p	109.0 p	109.4 p	110.8 p	111.0	105.7 p	95.5 p	106.9 p	111.6 p	93.7 p	99.1 p	105.0 p	112.4 p	111.6

Note: The dagger symbol beside a figure indicates the earliest revised value for each series. Figures marked with a 'p' are provisional.

1 Index numbers are constructed on a net sector basis ie transactions within sector are excluded.

2 Index numbers are compiled exclusive of VAT. Revenue duties (on cigarettes, tobacco and alcoholic liquor) are included, as is duty on hydrocarbon oils.

Source: Central Statistical Office

From: Monthly Digest of Statistics, May 1994, Table 18.6

Definitions and sources

The household sector includes private trusts and individuals living in institutions as well as those living in households. It differs from the personal sector, as defined in the national accounts, in that it excludes unincorporated private businesses, private non-profit-making bodies serving persons, and funds of life assurance and pension schemes. More information is given in an article in *Economic Trends*, September 1981.

Household disposable income is equal to the total current income of the household sector *less* payment of United Kingdom taxes on income, employees' national insurance contributions, and contributions of employees to occupational pension schemes. It is revalued at constant prices by a deflator implied by estimates of total household expenditure at current and constant prices. This deflator is a modified form of the consumers' expenditure deflator.

For other sources see:

Guide to Official Statistics, 1990 edition (200 pages approximately, fully indexed) HMSO.

Inland Revenue Statistics, HMSO.
Family Spending, HMSO.

9.1 Average earnings index: all employees: main industrial sectors
Great Britain   Classified according to the Standard Industrial Classification 1980

	Whole economy (Divisions 0-9)			Manufacturing industries (Divisions 2-4)			Production industries (Divisions 1-4)			Service industries (Divisions 6-9)		
	Actual	Seasonally adjusted	Underlying rate	Actual	Seasonally adjusted	Underlying rate	Actual	Seasonally adjusted	Underlying rate	Actual	Seasonally adjusted	Underlying rate
1985=100												
1985	100.0			100.0			100 0			100.0		
1986	107.9			107.7			108.0			107.7		
1987	116.3			116.3			116.7			116.0		
1988	126.4			126.2			126.5			126.2		
1990=100												
1990	100.0			100.0			100.0			100.2		
1991	108.0			108.2			108.6			107.7		
1992	114.6			115.3			115.8			114.1		
1991 Feb	104.1	105.4	9.25	104.5	105.2	8.75	104.8	105.6	9.00	103.7	105.0	9.00
Mar	106.5	105.7	9.00	106.1	105.8	8.50	106.2	106.2	9.00	106.9	105.6	8.75
Apr	106.4	106.5	8.75	107.6	106.7	8.50	107.6	107.0	9.00	105.6	105.9	8.25
May	107.0	107.2	8.50	107.4	107.0	8.75	108.2	107.9	9.00	106.5	106.7	8.00
Jun	107.9	107.3	8.00	109.0	107.8	8.25	109.1	108.1	8.75	107.1	106.7	7.50
Jul	109.0	107.8	7.75	109.3	108.1	8.25	109.5	108.3	8.50	108.5	107.6	7.50
Aug	109.2	109.8	7.75	108.2	109.8	8.00	109.0	110.0	8.25	109.2	109.6	7.50
Sep	109.3	110.0	7.75	108.6	109.8	8.00	109.6	110.6	8.00	109.0	109.8	7.50
Oct	109.3	110.2	7.50	110.0	110.8	8.00	110.3	111.0	8.50	108.8	110.0	7.25
Nov	111.4	111.0	7.50	111.5	111.3	8.00	112.0	111.7	8.25	111.2	111.0	7.25
Dec	112.3	110.5	7.25	112.7	111.6	7.75	112.9	111.9	8.00	111.9	109.5	7.00
1992 Jan	111.1	111.9	7.25	111.6	112.5	7.75	112.1	113.0	7.75	110.8	111.8	7.00
Feb	111.9	113.3	7.50	112.6	113.4	8.25	113.1	113.9	8.25	111.7	113.0	7.25
Mar	115.8	114.9	7.25	117.0	116.7	7.75	117.2	117.2	7.75	115.3	113.9	7.25
Apr	113.0	113.1	7.00	113.0	112.1	7.50	113.8	113.1	7.50	112.8	113.1	7.00
May	113.9	114.1	6.25	114.8	114.4	6.25	115.3	115.0	6.50	113.4	113.6	6.50
Jun	114.5	113.8	6.25	115.4	114.2	6.25	115.8	114.8	6.50	113.8	113.4	6.25
Jul	115.1	113.9	6.00	116.1	114.8	6.25	116.6	115.2	6.50	114.5	113.5	6.00
Aug	114.6	115.3	5.75	115.3	116.9	6.00	115.6	116.7	6.25	114.3	114.7	5.25
Sep	114.7	115.4	5.50	114.9	116.1	6.00	115.3	116.4	6.00	114.3	115.2	5.50
Oct	116.0	117.0	5.25	116.9	117.8	5.75	117.3	118.1	5.75	115.4	116.7	5.25
Nov	116.4	116.1	5.00	117.7	117.6	5.75	118.2	117.9	5.75	115.8	115.6	4.75
Dec	117.9	116.0	4.75	118.8	117.5	5.50	119.2	118.2	5.50	117.4	114.9	4.50
1993 Jan	116.1	117.0	4.75	117.1	118.1	5.25	117.6	118.6	5.25	115.6	116.7	4.50
Feb	116.7	118.2	4.50	118.3	119.2	5.00	118.7	119.6	5.00	116.1	117.5	4.25
Mar	119.6	118.7	4.00	121.9	121.6	5.00	122.1	122.2	5.00	118.5	117.1	3.75
Apr	117.5	117.6	4.00	119.0	118.0	5.00	119.7	118.9	5.00	116.5	116.8	3.25
May	118.0	118.3	3.75	120.3	119.9	5.00	120.8	120.4	5.00	116.9	117.0	3.00
Jun	118.5	117.8	3.75	121.0	119.6	5.00	121.3	120.2	5.00	117.0	116.5	2.75
Jul	119.5	118.3	3.75	121.9	120.5	4.75	122.4	121.0	4.75	118.3	117.3	2.75
Aug	118.2	118.9	3.25	119.5	121.1	4.50	119.9	121.0	4.50	117.3	117.7	2.75
Sep	118.0	118.8	3.00	120.1	121.4	4.25	120.6	121.7	4.50	116.8	117.7	2.25
Oct	118.4	119.4	3.00	121.3	122.3	4.25	121.7	122.6	4.25	116.9	118.2	2.25
Nov	120.0	119.7	3.00	122.4	122.3	4.25	123.1	122.7	4.25	118.7	118.5	2.50
Dec	121.6	119.6	3.25	123.6	122.3	4.25	124.1	123.0	4.25	120.8	118.3	2.75
1994 Jan	120.3	121.2	3.50	122.7	123.7	4.50	123.3	124.2	4.50	119.2	120.3	3.25
Feb	121.9	123.4	3.50	123.5	124.3	4.50	123.8	124.8	4.50	121.6	123.1	3.25

Note: The seasonal adjustment factors currently used for the SIC 1980 series are based on data up to April 1991.
For a detailed account of the revised Average Earnings Index based on 1990=100 please see the article in *Employment Gazette* November 1989 p.606-612.
Source: Department of Employment

From: Monthly Digest of Statistics, May 1994, Table 18.11
Key Data 94, © Crown copyright 1994

9.2 Real[1] weekly earnings[2] after income tax, national insurance contributions, child benefit and family credit: by selected family type

Great Britain £ per week[1]

	1971	1981	1991	1992
Single man, no children				
Lowest decile point	98.9	108.0	130.9	134.6
Median	146.3	160.3	211.3	217.6
Highest decile point	231.4	261.0	380.9	390.6
Single woman, no children				
Lowest decile point	63.4	80.6	103.5	107.5
Median	88.5	111.4	155.0	161.7
Highest decile point	138.1	180.7	263.5	277.8
Married man[3], no children				
Lowest decile point	106.1	116.3	139.5	142.9
Median	153.5	168.6	219.9	225.8
Highest decile point	238.6	269.4	389.5	402.2
Married man[3], 2 children[4]				
Lowest decile point[5]				
Family credit claimed	124.3	134.8	164.3	168.7
Family credit not claimed[6]	124.3	134.8	156.4	160.3
Median	171.6	187.1	236.8	243.3
Highest decile point	256.7	287.8	406.3	419.6

1 At April 1992 prices.
2 Figures relate to April each year and to full-time employees on adult rates whose pay for the survey pay-period was not affected by absence.
3 Assuming no wife's earnings.
4 Aged under 11.
5 In years up to 1987, there was no entitlement to Family Income Supplement for this category.
6 Families with capital of more than £3 000 would only be eligible to receive reduced amounts of family credit, or may not be eligible at all.

Source: Inland Revenue; Department of Social Security

From: Social Trends 1994, Table 5.13

9.3 Percentage of personal income taken by direct taxes and social security contributions[1]: international comparison, 1990

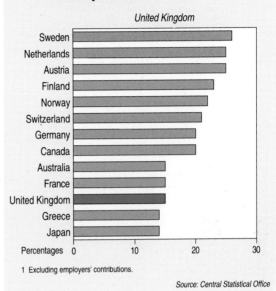

United Kingdom

Sweden · Netherlands · Austria · Finland · Norway · Switzerland · Germany · Canada · Australia · France · United Kingdom · Greece · Japan

Percentages 0 10 20 30

1 Excluding employers' contributions.

Source: Central Statistical Office

From: Social Trends 1994, Chart 5.14

INCOMES

9.4 Percentage of income paid in income tax and national insurance contributions[1]: by marital status and level of earnings[2]

United Kingdom   Percentages

	1971-72	1981-82	1991-92	1993-94[3]
Single person				
Half average earnings				
Tax	14.3	17.5	12.8	11.5
NIC	7.7	7.7	6.2	6.2
Average earnings				
Tax	22.2	23.7	18.9	18.3
NIC	5.8	7.7	7.6	7.6
Twice average earnings				
Tax	26.2	27.3	22.0	22.7
NIC	3.3	6.1	6.0	6.0
Married man[4]				
Half average earnings				
Tax	7.5	10.5	6.5	5.9
NIC	7.7	7.7	6.2	6.2
Average earnings				
Tax	18.8	20.2	15.7	15.3
NIC	5.8	7.7	7.6	7.6
Twice average earnings				
Tax	26.8	25.1	20.4	20.4
NIC	3.3	6.1	6.0	6.0

1 Employees' contributions. Assumes contributions at Class 1, contracted in, standard rate.
2 Average earnings for full-time adult male manual employees working a full week on adult rates.
3 1992-93 based projections.
4 Assuming wife not in paid employment.

Source: Inland Revenue
From: Social Trends 1994, Table 5.12

9.5 Composition of quintile groups of household income: by occupational group of head of household, 1991

United Kingdom   Percentages

	Quintile groups of households ranked by equivalised disposable income[1]					All house-holds
	Bottom fifth	Next fifth	Middle fifth	Next fifth	Top fifth	
Occupational group of head of household						
Professional	–	1	4	7	14	5
Employers and managers	3	4	9	17	34	13
Intermediate and junior non-manual	3	7	14	21	22	13
Skilled manual	10	17	27	26	15	19
Semi-skilled manual	6	10	12	9	2	8
Unskilled manual	3	3	3	2	-	2
Retired	49	44	22	12	7	27
Unoccupied	25	15	9	6	4	12
Other[2]	-	-	1	1	1	1
All occupational groups	100	100	100	100	100	100

1 Equivalised disposable income has been used for ranking the households into quintile groups; see Appendix, Part 5: Equalisation scales.
2 Mainly armed forces.

Source: Central Statistical Office, from the Family Expenditure Survey

From: Social Trends 1994, Table 5.17

Key Data 94, © Crown copyright 1994

9.6 Household income[1]

United Kingdom										Percentages and £ billion
	1971	1976	1981	1986	1987	1988	1989	1990	1991	1992
Source of income (percentages)										
Wages and salaries[2]	68	67	63	59	59	59	59	58	58	57
Income from self-employment[3]	9	9	8	10	10	11	11	11	10	9
Rent, dividends, interest	6	6	7	8	8	8	9	10	9	8
Private pensions, annuities, etc	5	5	6	8	9	8	8	8	10	11
Social security benefits	10	11	13	13	12	11	11	10	11	12
Other current transfers[4]	2	2	2	3	3	3	2	2	2	3
Total household income										
(= 100%) (£ billion)	44.7	100.4	202.1	313.9	341.4	376.3	422.0	472.7	500.9	529.5
Direct taxes etc (percentages of total household income)										
Taxes on income	14	17	14	14	14	14	14	14	14	13
National insurance contributions[5]	3	3	3	4	4	4	4	3	3	3
Contributions to pension schemes	1	2	2	2	2	2	2	2	2	2
Total household disposable income (£ billion)	36.4	78.3	162.4	251.9	275.0	302.8	340.6	382.5	408.3	435.2

1 See Appendix, Part 5: The household sector.
2 Includes Forces' pay and income in kind.
3 After deducting interest payments, depreciation and stock appreciation.
4 Mostly other government grants, but including transfers from abroad and from non-profit-making bodies.
5 By employees and the self-employed.

Source: Central Statistical Office

From: Social Trends 1994, Table 5.3

9.7 Real household disposable income per head

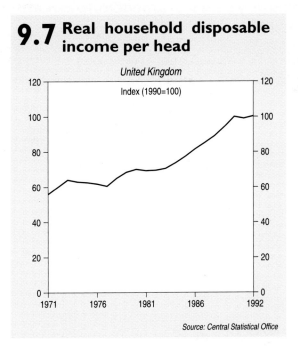

United Kingdom

Index (1990=100)

Source: Central Statistical Office

Source: Central Statistical Office

From: Social Trends 1994, Chart 5.2

9.8 Average weekly household disposable income per head: by region, 1991

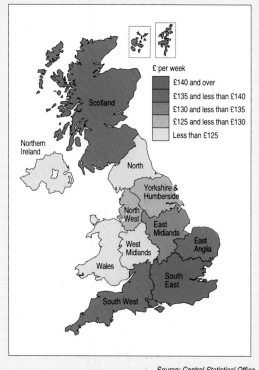

£ per week

- £140 and over
- £135 and less than £140
- £130 and less than £135
- £125 and less than £130
- Less than £125

Source: Central Statistical Office

From: Social Trends 1994, Chart 5.4

9.9 Non-contributory benefits-expenditure in real terms[1] and recipients[2]: by type of benefit

Great Britain

£ million at 1992-93 prices[1] and thousands

	Expenditure (£ million at 1992-93 prices[1])				Recipients[2] (thousands)			
	1976-77	1981-82	1991-92	1992-93	1976-77	1981-82	1991-92	1992-93
Non-income-related benefits								
Child benefit[3]	1 914	6 217	5 371	5 767	6 915	13 145	12 205	12 485
One-parent benefit	.	140	258	277	.	470	835	895
Non-contributory retirement pension	127	72	37	36	80	50	30	30
Industrial disablement benefit	588	581	608	596	.	.	295	295
Industrial death benefit	91	87	66	63	.	.	25	25
War pension	996	883	871	968	415	345	280	310
Attendance allowance	401	608	1 766	1 458	230	350	975	765
Invalid care allowance[4]	7	11	295	366	5	5	170	195
Severe disablement allowance[4]	120	240	617	652	105	180	305	320
Mobility allowance	28	319	1 099	125	30	210	665	.
Disability living allowance	.	.	.	1 095	.	.	.	935
Disability working allowance	.	.	.	4	.	.	.	5
Lump sum payment to non-contributory pensioners	.	11	11	12	.	600	1 100	1 200
Income-related benefits								
Supplementary pension	2 016	2 614	.	.	1 675	1 740	.	.
Supplementary allowance	4 011	6 309	.	.	1 305	1 985	.	.
Income support	.	.	12 054	14 461	.	.	4 660	5 320
Family income supplement	63	122	.	.	70	125	.	.
Family credit	.	.	648	864	.	.	355	420
Maternity grant	53	29	.	.	..	..	.	.
Housing benefit-rent rebates and allowances[4]	707	1 036	2 672	3 520	..	1 840	4 110	4 315
Rate rebates/community charge benefit	.	.	1 112	1 451	..	.	6 335	6 655
Social Fund[5]	.	.	217	231	.	.	..	..
Administration and miscellaneous service[6]	2 009	918	2 148	2 462	.	.	.	.

1 Expressed in real terms using the GDP deflator.
2 Estimated average number receiving benefit at any one time, except for lump sum payments, maternity grant and social fund payments which, because they are single payments, are the total number paid in each year.
3 Child benefit recipients relate to the number of qualifying children except for 1976-77 which relates to the number of qualifying families. In 1976-77 tax allowances were the main comparable form of child support.
4 There have been a number of changes to the system of assistance with housing costs. In particular, from 1990-91 most rent rebate expenditure is accounted for by the Department of the Environment and the Welsh Office, and is therefore not included.
5 Net expenditure after repayment of loans.
6 1976-77 figure represents administration cost of both contributory and non-contributory benefits.

Source: Department of Social Security
From: Social Trends 1994, Table 5.9

Key Data 94, © Crown copyright 1994

Definitions and sources

Differences in the legal and judicial systems of England and Wales, Scotland and Northern Ireland make it impossible to aggregate statistics for the United Kingdom as a whole.

In England and Wales, indictable offences include those which must be tried in the Crown Court and those which may be tried at a magistrates' court or in the Crown Court, although most are actually tried at a magistrates' court. Notifiable offences recorded by the police have a slightly wider definition than indictable offences in that, for example, they also include all criminal damage however small. Standard list offences include all indictable offences plus some summary offences but exclude most summary motoring offences and other less serious summary offences such as drunkenness. For other sources see:

Guide to Official Statistics, 1990 edition (200 pages approximately, fully indexed) HMSO.

10.1 Notifiable offences recorded by the police

England and Wales

Thousands

	Violence against the person	Sexual offences	Burglary	Robbery	Theft and handling stolen goods	Fraud and forgery	Criminal damage	Other	Total
1987	141.0	25.2	900.1	32.6	2 052.0	133.0	589.0	19.3	3 892.2
1988	158.2	26.5	817.8	31.4	1 931.3	133.9	593.9	22.7	3 715.8
1989	177.0	29.7	825.9	33.2	2 012.8	134.5	630.1	27.6	3 870.7
1990	184.7	29.0	1 006.8	36.2	2 374.4	147.9	733.4	31.1	4 543.6
1991	190.3	29.4	1 219.5	45.3	2 761.1	174.7	821.1	34.6	5 276.2
1992	201.8	29.5	1 355.3	52.9	2 851.6	168.6	892.6	39.4	5 591.7
1993	205.4	31.4	1 370.0	58.3	2 753.9	163.1	907.2	41.0	5 530.4
1988 Q4	42.7	6.3	206.1	8.1	479.1	31.8	151.4	6.1	931.6
1989 Q1	39.3	7.0	213.3	8.2	479.6	32.1	156.8	6.0	942.2
Q2	45.2	7.5	192.7	7.8	499.1	32.8	156.0	6.6	947.8
Q3	48.3	8.0	192.3	8.0	505.2	35.4	152.5	7.3	957.0
Q4	44.2	7.2	227.7	9.1	528.8	34.2	164.8	7.8	1 023.8
1990 Q1	41.0	6.6	252.3	8.4	555.2	34.7	175.4	7.2	1 080.9
Q2	47.0	7.4	231.6	8.4	586.3	34.4	188.6	7.8	1 111.3
Q3	49.5	7.9	233.4	8.9	590.5	37.3	175.0	7.7	1 110.3
Q4	47.2	7.2	289.5	10.5	642.4	41.4	194.4	8.4	1 241.0
1991 Q1	41.6	6.6	298.9	9.6	649.3	41.4	195.6	8.2	1 251.2
Q2	48.1	7.6	292.0	10.7	701.1	44.1	214.0	8.5	1 326.2
Q3	52.3	8.1	289.3	11.8	703.8	44.9	195.8	8.9	1 315.0
Q4	48.3	7.1	339.2	13.2	706.9	44.4	215.8	9.0	1 383.8
1992 Q1	45.5	7.2	347.5	12.0	704.6	42.4	223.8	9.9	1 392.9
Q2	53.4	7.4	313.9	12.4	716.5	42.9	220.5	9.7	1 376.7
Q3	53.1	7.8	316.4	13.6	707.5	42.7	212.1	10.3	1 363.4
Q4	49.8	7.1	377.5	14.8	723.1	40.7	236.3	9.6	1 458.8
1993 Q1	47.2	6.7	380.7	14.2	708.9	42.0	239.6	9.0	1 448.2
Q2	53.2	7.9	336.5	13.7	714.2	41.9	229.2	9.7	1 406.3
Q3	54.1	8.8	315.6	15.2	687.8	41.9	214.9	11.1	1 349.4
Q4	50.9	7.9	337.2	15.2	643.1	37.3	223.6	11.1	1 326.2

Source: Home Office

From: Monthly Digest of Statistics, May 1994, Table 5.1

LAW

10.2 Crimes and offences recorded by the police[1,2]

Scotland

	Non-sexual crimes of violence	Crimes of indecency	Crimes of dishonesty	Fire raising, vandalism etc	Other crimes	Motor vehicle offences	Miscellaneous offences	Total crimes and offences (monthly)	Total crimes and offences (annual)
1986	15.7	5.4	342.5	78.9	21.4	238.1	120. 4	823.5	822.4
1987	18.5	5.2	356.7	76.6	24.4	249.6	127. 2	858.3	858.2
1988	18.0	5.1	344.7	73.5	28.6	248.6	124. 9	843.5	855.6
1989	18.5	5.7	354.2	78.6	34.0	277.8	124. 8	893.6	902.0
1990	18.6	6.0	386.2	86.2	39.6	294.1	127. 2	957.9	959.1
1991	21.7	5.9	432.4	90.1	44.9	305.6	122. 7	1 023.0	1 020.7
1992	23.5	6.2	417.0	92.1	52.0	306.5	127. 8	1 025.4	1 023.5
1988 Q3	4.5	1.3	85.3	17.6	7.8	58.3	31.6	206.4	
Q4	4.6	1.2	90.4	19.3	7.9	65.0	31.9	220.3	
1989 Q1	4.4	1.2	84.9	19.0	7.1	69.7	27.7	214.0	
Q2	4.9	1.4	88.1	20.0	8.6	71.2	33.0	227.2	
Q3	4.7	1.6	89.4	19.2	8.3	64.6	32.4	220.2	
Q4	4.5	1.5	91.8	20.5	10.0	72.2	31.7	232.1	
1990 Q1	4.5	1.5	94.6	21.6	9.1	72.5	30.3	234.0	
Q2	4.5	1.7	92.5	21.4	9.8	75.0	32.8	237.7	
Q3	4.8	1.5	96.2	20.7	10.0	71.6	32.6	237.5	
Q4	4.8	1.4	102.9	22.5	10.7	75.0	31.5	248.7	
1991 Q1	4.7	1.3	97.6	21.9	10.0	77.9	28.3	241.7	
Q2	5.2	1.6	107.6	23.2	11.1	79.2	31.0	258.9	
Q3	5.7	1.6	111.4	21.8	11.8	73.3	32.3	257.8	
Q4	6.1	1.4	115.7	23.2	12.0	75.2	31.1	264.6	
1992 Q1	5.7	1.5	105.4	22.7	11.3	78.8	29.0	254.4	
Q2	6.5	1.6	106.8	24.4	13.0	77.2	33.3	262.8	
Q3	5.8	1.6	100.6	22.3	13.4	73.8	33.1	250.5	
Q4	5.5	1.5	104.2	23.0	14.3	76.7	32.4	257.7	
1993 Q1	5.1	1.5	92.1	21.7	12.8	72.3	29.2	234.7	
Q2	5.1	1.6	95.5	20.3	14.7	87.3	32.4	256.9	
Q3	5.0	1.6	92.7	21.2	15.9	76.6	33.6	246.6	

1 Components may not add to totals due to separate rounding.
2 Annual consolidate returns have been used to produce the yearly data. Quarterly data is obtained from monthly returns by police forces. Hence there might be slight differences when the the quarterly data is summed into years.

Source: The Scottish Office Home and Health Department
From: Monthly Digest of Statistics, May 1994, Table 5.2

10.3 Offenders sentenced for indictable offences: by type of offence and type of sentence, 1992

England & Wales

Percentages and thousands

	Discharge	Probation/ Supervision	Community service order	Fine	Fully suspended sentence	Immediate custody Under 5 years	Immediate custody 5 years and over	Other	Total sentenced (= 100%) (thousands)
Offences									
Violence against the person	24	9	10	26	7	16	1	8	43.6
Sexual offences	10	21	2	17	8	29	10	3	4.9
Burglary	12	20	17	12	6	27	-	6	44.3
Robbery	4	12	5	1	2	54	15	7	5.1
Theft and handling stolen goods	28	12	9	35	5	8	-	3	127.8
Fraud and forgery	25	10	12	27	10	12	-	3	20.1
Criminal damage	27	18	9	22	3	10	-	11	9.9
Drug offences	15	6	5	53	5	14	2	1	22.7
Motoring	5	5	7	68	3	13	0	1	10.7
Other	16	4	6	55	4	11	-	4	35.5
All indictable offences	21	11	10	34	5	14	1	4	324.6

Source: Home Office
From: Social Trends 1994, Table 12.22

Key Data 94, © Crown copyright 1994

10.4 Notifiable offences[1] recorded by the police: by type of offence

England & Wales, Scotland and Northern Ireland   Thousands

	England & Wales			Scotland			Northern Ireland		
	1981	1991	1992	1981	1991	1992	1981	1991[2]	1992[2]
Violence against the person	100.2	190.3	201.8	8.0	15.5	16.5	2.9	4.0	4.1
Sexual offences	19.4	29.4	29.5	2.1	3.1	3.3	0.3	0.9	1.0
of which: rape	1.1	4.0	4.1	0.3	0.5	0.5	-	0.1	0.1
Burglary	718.4	1 219.5	1 355.3	95.7	116.1	113.2	20.5	16.6	17.1
Robbery	20.3	45.3	52.9	4.2	6.2	6.8	2.7	1.8	1.9
Drug trafficking	..	11.4	13.8	1.6	3.3	4.1	-	-	0.1
Theft and handling stolen goods,	1 603.2	2 761.1	2 851.6	201.1	284.3	270.8	25.4	32.0	34.3
of which: theft of vehicles	332.6	581.9	585.5	32.5	44.3	47.4	5.1	8.4	9.4
theft from vehicles[3]	379.6	913.3	961.3	..	..	97.1	6.5	7.2	7.1
Fraud and forgery	106.7	174.7	168.6	21.4	26.4	27.7	2.6	4.8	5.4
Criminal damage[4]	386.7	821.1	892.6	61.7	89.7	92.2	5.2	2.4	2.5
Other notifiable offences	8.9	23.2	25.6	12.4	48.1	55.0	2.8	1.0	1.2
Total notifiable offences	2 963.8	5 276.2	5 591.7	408.2	592.8	589.6	62.5	63.5	67.5

1 Includes attempted offences. Scottish figures of 'crime' have been recompiled to approximate to the classification of notifiable offences in England and Wales and Northern Ireland. However, because of differences in the legal system, recording and counting practices and classification problems, Scottish figures are not comparable with those for England & Wales and Northern Ireland.

2 These figures no longer include assault on police and communicating false information regarding a bomb hoax. These offences have been removed from the categories 'Violence against the person' and 'Other notifiable offences'.

3 In Scotland, data have only been collected from January 1992. The figures include theft by opening lockfast places from motor vehicles and other theft from vehicles.

4 In Northern Ireland, the figures exclude criminal damage valued at £200 or less.

Sources: Home Office; The Scottish Office Home and Health Department; Royal Ulster Constabulary

From: Social Trends 1994, Table 12.2

10.5 Drug offences, persons found guilty, cautioned or dealt with by compounding[1]: by type of offence

United Kingdom   Numbers

	1981	1986	1991	1992
Unlawful production[2]	1 603	944	664	756
Unlawful supply	1 000	1 876	2 133	2 189
Possession with intent to supply unlawfully	699	1 858	2 782	3 203
Unlawful possession	14 850	20 052	42 575	43 492
Unlawful import or export	1 357	1 525	2 136	2 034
All drug offences[3]	17 921	23 905	47 616	48 927

1 Includes HM Customs and Excise cases dealt with by the payment of a penalty in lieu of prosecution.

2 Includes offences of cultivation of cannabis plants.

3 As the same person may appear in more than one category, rows cannot be added together to produce totals or sub-totals.

Source: Home Office

From: Social Trends 1994, Table 12.18

LAW

10.6 Population[1] in custody in prison establishments

United Kingdom				Thousands
	1981	1986	1991	1992
Average population				
Males	48.9	52.5	49.7	50.0
Females	1.6	1.8	1.7	1.8
Total	50.5	54.3	51.4	51.8
Remand prisoners				
Untried prisoners	5.9	9.6	.8.6	8.6
Convicted prisoners awaiting sentence[2]	2.3	1.7	2.0	2.1
All remand prisoners	8.2	11.3	10.6	10.7
Sentenced prisoners				
Adults	29.3	32.0	33.7	34.3
Young offenders[3]	12.6	10.7	6.8	6.5
Other sentences	-	-	0.1	0.1
All sentenced prisoners	41.9	42.7	40.6	40.9
Non-criminal prisoners	0.4	0.2	0.3	0.3

1 Annual averages. Excludes prisoners held in police cells in England and Wales.
2 Includes persons remanded in custody while social and medical inquiry reports are prepared prior to sentence. Prisoners in Northern Ireland are not committed for sentence but are sentenced at the court of conviction.
3 See Appendix in *Social Trends*, Part 12: Young offenders.

Sources: Home Office ; The Scottish Office Home and Health Department; Northern Ireland Office

From: Social Trends 1994, Table 12.27

10.7 Prison population[1] rates: by ethnic origin

England & Wales	Rate per 10,000 population[2]		
	Males	Females	All
White	19.4	0.5	9.6
West Indian, Guyanese, African	144.0	9.9	76.7
Indian, Pakistani, Bangladeshi	24.3	0.4	12.4
Other/not disclosed	72.1	5.4	38.3
All ethnic origins	22.0	0.7	11.0

1 On June 30, 1992.
2 Aged 14 and over.

Sources: Home Office; Office of Population Censuses and Surveys

From: Social Trends 1994, Table 12.28

10.8 Average population in custody[1]:by type of prisoner

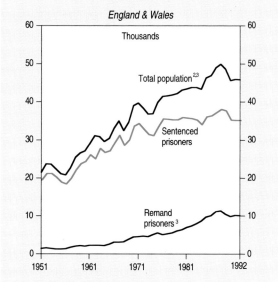

1 Includes those held in police cells because of shortage of accommodation.
2 Includes a small number of non-criminal prisoners.
3 Including those in police cells from 1980.

Source: Home Office

From: Social Trends 1994, Chart 12.26

52

Key Data 94, © Crown copyright 1994

10.9 Sentenced prisoners[1]: by sex and length of sentence

United Kingdom

	1986	1988	1989	1990	1991	1992
Males						
Prisoners aged under 21 serving[2]:						
Up to 18 months	6 789	5 235	4 213	3 682	3 540	3 392
Over 18 months and up to 4 years	2 732	3 172	2 839	2 522	2 189	2 271
Over 4 years, less than Life	646	889	849	804	712	633
Life sentences	271	227	212	207	169	144
Prisoners aged 21 and over serving:						
Up to 18 months	11 388	10 268	9 442	8 309	8 941	10 550
Over 18 months and up to 4 years	9 900	11 255	11 606	10 058	9 634	9 517
Over 4 years, less than Life	6 779	9 000	9 877	10 294	10 670	9 933
Life sentences	2 670	3 022	3 189	3 279	3 397	3 486
All sentenced male prisoners[3]	41175	43 067	42 227	39 154	39 253	39 925
Females						
Prisoners of all ages serving:						
Up to 18 months	810	613	558	532	497	559
Over 18 months and up to 4 years	355	480	453	398	331	329
Over 4 years, less than Life	134	227	295	336	348	330
Life sentences	80	89	97	102	106	105
All sentenced female prisoners[3]	1 379	1 410	1 404	1 369	1 281	1 323

1 As at 30 June each year for England & Wales and annual averages for Scotland and Northern Ireland.
2 For Scotland includes detention centre sentences which were abolished on 1 November 1988.
3 Excludes prisoners held in police cells in England and Wales.

Sources: *Home Office; The Scottish Office Home and Health Department, Northern Ireland Office*

From: *Social Trends 1994, Table 12.29*

Definitions and sources

The traffic figures for Great Britain were revised in 1989 (see *Road Traffic in Great Britain: Review of Estimates, Transport Statistics Report HMSO 1989*). The figures are compiled using roadside traffic counts from which estimates of average daily flow are made. These are combined with information on road lengths to provide estimates of traffic volume in terms of vehicle kilometres.

For other sources see:

Guide to Official Statistics, 1990 edition (200 pages approximately, fully indexed) HMSO.

Transport Statistics, Great Britain HMSO.

11.1 Road vehicles in Great Britain: new registrations by taxation class

Thousands

	Private and light goods[1]		Motor cycles, scooters and rnopeds	Goods vehicles l	Public transport vehicles	Agricultural tractors[2]	Other vehicles[3]	Total	Of which body-type cars		
	Private cars	Other vehicles							Total	Percent company	Percent imported
1987	1 962.7	248.3	90.8	54.0	8.7	37.7	70.1	2 473.9	2 016.2	48	50
1988	2 154.7	282.3	90.1	63.4	9.2	45.6	78.6	2 723.5	2 210.3	51	55
1989	2 241.2	294.0	97.3	64.7	8.0	42.5	81.4	2 828.9	2 304.4	51	55
1990	1 942.3	237.6	94.4	44.0	7.4	34.2	78.4	2 438.4	2 005.1	52	56
1991	1 536.6	171.9	76.5	28.6	5.2	26.1	76.6	1 921.5	1 600.1	52	55
1993 Mar	152.2	14.7	5.7	2.5	0.7	2.7	9.0	187.6	159.8	55	55
Apr	127.3	13.8	6.1	2.4	0.5	2.6	7.2	160.0	133.4	58	54
May	128.8	12.2	6.3	2.4	0.4	2.6	7.2	160.0	135.0	59	53
Jun	105.6	11.7	5.6	2.6	0.4	2.1	7.6	135.2	111.8	58	55
Jul	33.7	5.8	3.3	1.2	0.2	1.4	3.6	49.2	36.6	56	55
Aug	424.4	26.4	10.6	4.6	0.7	5.5	17.9	490.0	441.1	41	59
Sep	128.0	12.6	4.7	4.5	0.6	2.8	7.8	161.0	134.8	49	57
Oct	121.5	13.4	3.5	2.6	0.4	2.7	7.8	152.0	128.5	52	55
Nov	122.2	13.4	2.9	3.2	0.4	2.5	7.4	152.0	128.8	53	55
Dec	72.1	8.2	2.0	2.4	0.4	1.4	5.3	91.6	76.6	58	53
1994 Jan	190 0	15.6	3.8	2.3	0.4	2.1	7.8	222.0	196.8	54	55
Feb	137.0	13.0	4.7	2.7	0.8	2.4	8.5	169.2	144.7	54	57
Mar	172.9	18.3	6.2	3.7	0.7	3.4	10.1	215.3	181.6	55	58

1 For the period up to Oct 1990 retrospective counts within these taxation classes have been estimated. See notes and definitions on taxation class changes.

2 Includes trench diggers, mobile cranes etc but excludes agricultural tractors on exempt licences.

3 Includes crown and exempt vehicles, three-wheelers, pedestrian controlled vehicles, general haulage and showmen's tractors.

Source: Department of Transport

From: Monthly Digest of Statistics, May 1994, Table 13.1

11.2 Households with regular use of a car[1]

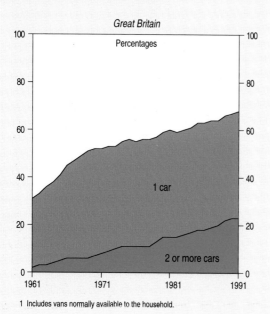

1 Includes vans normally available to the household.

Source: Department of Transport

From: Social Trends 1994, Chart 13.11

Key Data 94, © Crown copyright 1994

11.3 Road and rail passenger transport use

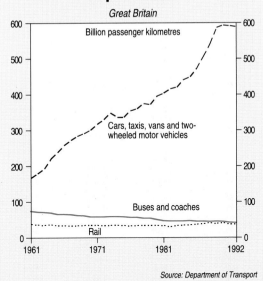

Great Britain

Source: Department of Transport

From: Social Trends 1994, Chart 13.3

11.4 Road casualties in Great Britain

Number

	Total casualties		Severity			All severities			
	All ages	Under 16 years	Killed	Seriously injured	Slightly injured	Pedestrians	Pedal cyclists	Motor cyclists and their passengers[1]	Other drivers and their passengers
1987	311 473	40 013	5 125	64 293	242 055	57 453	26 194	45 801	182 025
1988	322 305	41 050	5 052	63 491	253 762	58 843	25 849	42 836	194 777
1989	341 592	43 041	5 373	63 158	273 061	60 080	28 513	42 630	210 369
1990	341 141	48 640	5 217	60 441	275 483	60 230	26 422	39 042	215 447
1991	311 269	44 409	4 568	51 605	255 096	53 992	24 803	30 736	201 738
1992	310 673	44 186	4 229	49 245	257 199	51 587	24 755	26 873	207 458
1993	305 556	42 482	3 819	44 891	256 845	48 067	24 100	25 052	208 388
1990 Q4	88 553	10 378	1 418	15 371	71 764	15 402	5 821	9 138	58 192
1991 Q1	70 217	8 962	969	11 746	57 502	12 817	4 643	6 040	46 717
Q2	77 702	12 673	1 047	12 921	63 734	13 638	6 586	8 178	49 300
Q3	81 667	13 241	1 203	13 580	66 884	13 276	8 304	9 248	50 839
Q4	81 683	9 533	1 349	13 358	66 976	14 261	5 270	7 270	54 882
1992 Q1	71 756	8 872	971	11 238	59 547	12 300	4 738	5 601	49 117
Q2	75 395	12 775	1 004	12 335	62 056	12 874	7 179	7 382	47 960
Q3	80 185	12 425	1 078	12 815	66 292	12 036	7 299	7552	53 298
Q4	83 337	10 114	1 176	12 857	69 304	14 377	5 539	6338	57 083
1993 Q1[2]	66 326	8 304	837	9 874	55 615	11 378	4 605	5 072	45 271
Q2[2]	76 099	11 942	889	11 278	63 931	11 710	6 768	6 806	50 816
Q3[2]	79 348	12 466	951	11 526	66 871	11 617	7 380	7 143	53 258
Q4[2]	83 783	9 770	1 142	12 213	70 428	13 362	5 347	6 031	59 043

1 Includes riders and passengers of mopeds, motor scooters and combinations.
2 Provisional.

Sources: Department of Transport;
Scottish Development Department;
Welsh Office

From: Monthly Digest of Statistics, May 1994, Table 13.4

11.5 Local (stage) bus services: fare indices
Great Britain

1985=100

	London	English metropolitan areas	English shire counties	England	Scotland	All Great Britain	All outside London	All outside London and English metropolitan areas
1988/89[1]	125.3	146.7	117.6	127.0	112.2	124.3	124.2	115.9
1989/90[1]	138.2	158.7	127.3	137.8	117.9	134.3	133.6	124.7
1990/91[1]	152.5	176.4	140.5	152.1	126.9	147.8	147.0	136.9
1991/92[1]	166.9	197.0	151.4	165.9	136.6	160.8	159.8	147.6
1992/93[1]	179.8	210.7	157.9	175.1	146.0	170.1	168.4	154.9
1989 Q4	136.1	160.0	128.5	138.3	118.6	134.8	134.6	125.6
1990 Q1	144.6	161.9	131.2	141.9	119.6	138.1	136.9	128.1
Q2	148.8	166.1	135.6	146.1	122.6	142.0	140.9	132.1
Q3	148.8	171.4	137.9	148.8	124.5	144.6	143.9	134.2
Q4	148.8	181.4	142.8	154.0	128.7	149.7	149.8	139.0
1991 Q1	163.4	186.7	145.6	159.5	131.9	154.8	153.3	142.1
Q2	163.8	191.5	148.1	162.1	134.3	157.4	156.3	144.6
Q3	164.0	194.6	150.3	164.1	136.1	159.3	158.5	146.6
Q4	164.0	199.6	152.9	166.8	136.3	161.5	161.2	148.6
1992 Q1	176.0	202.2	154.2	170.4	139.8	165.1	163.2	150.6
Q2	176.0	207.3	156.0	172.4	144.9	167.7	166.3	153.2
Q3	176.0	209.1	157.0	173.4	145.4	168.5	167.4	154.0
Q4	176.0	212.1	159.0	175.2	146.1	170.1	169.3	155.6
1993 Q1	191.3	214.3	159.6	179.6	147.6	174.0	170.6	156.6
Q2	191.3	218.8	160.5	181.3	149.5	175.7	172.7	157.8
Q3	191.3	219.5	161.1	181.8	150.2	176.2	173.4	158.4
Q4[2]	191.3	220.9	163.1	183.1	151.3	177.5	175.0	160.2

1 Due to rounding financial year data may differ slightly from that published by the Department of Transport.
2 Provisional.

Source: Department of Transport
From: Monthly Digest of Statistics, May 1994, Table 13.6

11.6 Index numbers of road traffic and goods transport by road

Average 1977=100

	Index of vehicle kilometres travelled on roads in Great Britain[1]								Index of tonne-kilo-metres of road goods transport[4,5,6]
	Motor traffic					Other goods vehicles		Pedal cycles	
	All motor traffic	Motorcycles etc	Cars and taxis	Buses and coaches	Light vans[2]	Total	Articulated[3]		
1987	142	108	147	126	131	120	144	95	114
1988	152	97	157	134	145	129	158	86	131
1989	165	96	171	140	160	137	174	86	139
1990	166	90	173	142	161	134	171	87	137
1991	166	87	173	149	168	134	171	86	131
1992	165	73	172	142	165	131	164	78	128
1993[7]	164	-	172	-	163	129	-	-	-
1991 Q1	152	71	157	136	161	128	170	53	131
Q2	172	97	178	161	175	138	174	86	134
Q3	179	110	186	161	179	140	170	119	132
Q4	162	71	170	149	157	129	166	79	127
1992 Q1	155	57	163	136	150	124	160	61	126
Q2	172	86	179	149	178	134	167	96	132
Q3	176	84	183	151	178	139	168	86	129
Q4	158	64	165	130	154	126	165	67	123
1993 Q1[7]	150	-	157	-	143	120	-	-	138
Q2[7]	168	-	176	-	166	126	-	-	133
Q3[7]	176	-	183	-	178	139	-	-	135
Q4[7]	164	-	173	-	166	132	-	-	135
1994 Q1	..	..	..	..	..	..	..	..	141

1 All indices have been revised.
2 Not exceeding 3 500 kgs gross vehicle weight.
3 Includes vehicles with drawbar trailers.
4 The figures for road goods transport are estimated from a continuing sample enquiry.
5 The quarterly figures relate to 13-week periods and not three calendar months.
6 Revised to exclude estimates of work done by vehicles under 3.5 tonnes gross vehicle weight.
7 Index of vehicle kilometres is provisional for 1993.

Source: Department of Transport
From: Monthly Digest of Statistics, May 1994, Table 13.3

Key Data 94, © Crown copyright 1994

11.7 British Rail and London Underground

Millions

	British Rail: passenger kilometres			London Underground: passenger journeys[2]		
	Ordinary fares	Season tickets	Total	Full and reduced fares	Season tickets	Total
1989	22 629	10 766	33 394	380	385	765
1990	23 463	10 762	34 226	399	376	775
1991	22 186	10 030	32 216	368	383	751
1992	22 184	9 578	31 732	365	363	728
1993	21 491	9 043	30 533	..	..	..
1989 Q4	5 983	2 852	8 834	101	100	201
1990 Q1	5 444	2 986	8 430	96	99	195
Q2	5 868	2 526	8 394	101	94	195
Q3	6 327	2 400	8 726	105	95	200
Q4	5 825	2 851	8 675	102	96	198
1991 Q1	4 784	2 612	7 396	90	92	182
Q2	5 548	2 502	8 050	92	97	188
Q3	6 186	2 265	8 451	96	94	190
Q4	5 668	2 651	8 319	94	95	190
1992 Q1	5 033	2 614	7 646	86	97	183
Q2	5 646	2 295	7 941	90	90	179
Q3	6 034	2 172	8 206	97	88	185
Q4	5 442	2 497	7 938	92	92	185
1993 Q1	5 159	2 474	7 633	86	93	179
Q2[1]	5 167	2 101	7 268	90[3]	87[3]	177[3]
Q3	5 840	2 061	7 901	96[3]	89[3]	185[3]
Q4	5 325	2 407	7 732	95[3]	91[3]	186[3]

1 NUR industrial action on 2 days (BR only).
2 From 1985 LRT annual figures relate to financial years.
3 Provisional.

Source: Department of Transport

From: Monthly Digest of Statistics, May 1994, Table 13.7

11.8 British Rail: freight traffic

	British Rail[1]				
	Freight lifted: million tonnes				
	Coal and coke	Metals including iron and steel	Other traffic	Total	Net tonne kilometres: millions
1989	76.5	19.7	47.2	143.4	17 247
1990	74.9	18.4	47.0	140.3	15 844
1991[2]	74.8	17.3	42.7	134.8	15 466
1992	68.8	16.6	39.8	125.2	15 253
1993	54.8	15.8	38.0	108.6	13 699
1989 Q4	19.5	4.4	12.1	36.0	4 357
1990 Q1	20.2	4.6	12.1	36.8	3 628
Q2	18.6	4.9	12.3	35.8	4 185
Q3	18.1	4.6	11.5	34.2	4 070
Q4	18.1	4.3	11.1	33.5	3 961
1991 Q1	20.0	4.2	10.4	34.6	3 784
Q2[2]	18.8	4.8	10.8	34.4	4 002
Q3[2]	17.8	4.0	10.8	32.6	3 892
Q4[2]	18.3	4.3	10.6	33.1	3 788
1992 Q1[2]	20.2	4.7	10.8	35.7	3 618
Q2	15.9	4.8	10.0	30.7	4 057
Q3	16.3	3.7	9.7	29.7	3 781
Q4	16.4	3.5	9.3	29.2	3 797
1993 Q1	19.3	3.9	9.6	32.8	3 851
Q2[3]	11.4	4.4	8.9	24.8	3 193
Q3	12.0	3.7	9.9	25.6	3 286
Q4	12.1	3.7	9.6	25.5	3 369

1 Freight train traffic only.
2 Net tonne-kilometres estimated by Department of Transport.
3 Industrial action on 2 days.

Source: Department of Transport

From: Monthly Digest of Statistics, May 1994, Table 13.8

11.9 UK airlines: aircraft kilometres flown, passengers and cargo uplifted
Tonne-kilometres and seat kilometres used on scheduled services

Monthly averages[1] or calendar rnonths: thousands or tonnes

	All services			Domestic services			International services		
	Aircraft kilometres flown (000's)	Passengers uplifted (000's)	Cargo uplifted (tonnes)[2]	Aircraft kilometres flown (000's)	Passengers uplifted (000's)	Cargo uplifted (tonnes)[2]	Aircr att kilometres flown (000's)	Passengers upliited	Cargo uplifted (tonnes)[2]
1985	30 955	2 068.7	30 003	5 772	747.7	3 842	25 183	1 321.0	26 161
1986	32 067	2 083.1	31 330	5 932	756.8	3 962	26 136	1 326.3	27 368
1987	33 802	2 374.7	33 780	6 127	837.4	4 235	27 675	1 537.3	29 546
1988	36 562	2 603.7	35 669	6 446	933.2	4 064	30 117	1 670.5	31 606
1989	40 472	2 931.0	37 786	7 100	1 019.2	3 888	33 372	1 911.8	33 898
1990	43 653	3 196.0	40 461	7 207	1 057.5	3 818	36 446	2138.5	36 643
1991	41 475	2 882.7	38 885	7 169	970.8	3 145	34 306	1911.9	35 740
1992 Dec	43 407	2 782.2	44 166	6 993	850.2	2 922	36 414	1 931.9	41 244
1993 Jan	44 639	2 680.8	38 262	6 931	781.9	2 354	37 708	1 898.8	35 908
Feb	40 667	2 585.1	40 067	6 725	788.5	2 379	33 942	1 796.5	37 688
Mar	45 758	3 168.3	45 439	7 697	967.1	2 752	38 061	2 201.2	42 687
Apr	47 797	3 394.6	41 887	7 588	1 033.5	2 594	40 209	2 361.1	39 293
May	50 218	3 425.1	46 244	7 801	1 048.7	2 440	42 417	2 376.3	43 804
Jun	49 892	3 577.7	42 955	8 168	1 093.8	2 568	41 724	2 483.9	40 387
Jul	53 222	3 888.7	46 141	8 578	1 143.6	2 530	44 644	2 745.0	43 611
Aug	52 636	3 923.0	44 692	8 543	1 154.6	2 408	44 093	2 768.4	42 284
Sep	51 466	3 799.7	46 446	8 379	1 163.5	2 634	43 087	2 636.1	43 812
Oct	51 510	3 638.9	50 644	8 076	1 070.5	2 551	43 434	2 568.4	48 093
Nov	47 473	3 003.4	49 879	7 387	923.2	2 636	40 086	2 080.3	47 243
Dec	47 424	3 002.9	49 348	7 166	913.6	2 827	40 258	2 089.3	46 521

Note: All kilometre statistics are based on standard (Great Circle) distance.
1 The annual figure is represented by the monthly average of passenger permitted baggage uplift.
2 Including weight of freight mail, excess baggage and diplomatic bags, but excluding passengers' and crews' permitted baggage.

Source: Civil Aviation Authority
From: Monthly Digest of Statistics, May 1994, Table 13.9

11.10 United Kingdom and Crown Dependency registered trading vessels of 500 gross tons and over[1]
Summary of tonnage by type

End of year

	1985	1986		1986	1991	1992
Number			**Number**			
Passenger[3]	83	79	Passenger[7]	8	8	9
Cargo liners	87	68	Container (FC)	47	32	28
Tramps	155	132	Other general cargo[6]	128	99	84
Bulk carriers	73	50	Bulk carriers4	73	32	30
Tankers	242	169	Tankers	165	124	108
Container (FC)	53	4	Specialised carriers	21	18	13
			Ro-ro[5]	104	96	91
All vessels	693	545	All vessels	546	409	363
Thousand gross tons			**Thousand gross tons**			
Passenger[3]	616	588	Passenger[7]	259	271	276
Cargo liners	728	564	Container (FC)	1 369	1 091	1 015
Tramps	335	244	Other general cargo[6]	510	242	174
Bulk carriers[2]	2 851	1 864	Bulk carriers[4]	2 003	489	446
Tankers	6 191	3 083	Tankers	3 249	2 166	2 188
Container (FC)	1 489	1 369	Specialised carriers	95	99	100
			Ro-ro[5]	561	604	632
All vessels	12 208	7 711	All vessels	8 046	4 963	4 831
Thousand deadweight tonnes			**Thousand deadweight tonnes**			
Passenger[3]	162	156	Passenger[7]	47	49	49
Cargo liners	1 002	748	Container (FC)	1 298	1 019	976
Tramps	527	395	Other general cargo	749	349	260
Bulk carriers[2]	5 072	3 321	Bulk carriers[4]	3 569	825	749
Tankers	10 378	5 499	Tankers	5 908	3 875	3 944
Container (FC)	1 395	1 284	Specialised carriers	122	81	84
All vessels	18 894	11 402	All vessels	12 073	6 477	6 335

1 In 1986 a new classification of ship types was introduced. This was based on ship descriptions used by Lloyd's Register of Shipping from which the Department of Transport has been taking figures data since 1986. Because of this change, figures for 1986 in Table 10.29 have been given on both bases.
2 Bulk carriers 10 000 deadweight tonnes and over or approximately 6 000 gross tons and over including combination ore/oil and ore/bulk/oil carriers.
3 All vessels with passenger certificates.
4 Bulk carriers (large and small) including combination ore/oil and ore/bulk/oil carriers.
5 Ro-ro passenger and cargo vessels.
6 General cargo roll-on/roll-off and lift-on/lift-off vessels, specialised dry cargo vessels and passenger ro-ro vessels.
7 Cruise liner and other passenger.

Source: Department of Transport
From: Annual Abstract of Statistics, Table 10.29
Key Data 94, © Crown copyright 1994

Definitions and sources

Most of the tables and charts in this section are taken from *Social Trends* 24 in which, in order to preserve topicality, almost a third of the tables and charts are new compared with the previous edition.

For other sources see:

Guide to Official Statistics, 1990 edition (200 pages approximately, fully indexed) HMSO.

12.1   Free time in a typical week: by sex and employment status, 1992-93

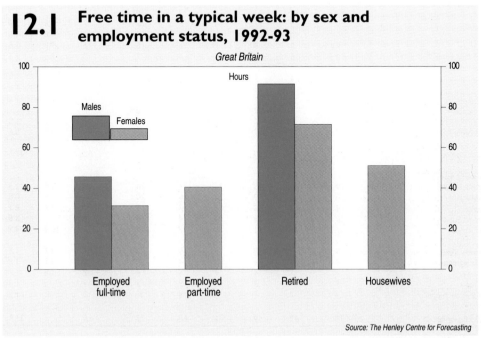

Source: The Henley Centre for Forecasting

From: Social Trends 1994, Chart 10.1

12.2   Video cassette recorders and hiring of pre-recorded tapes

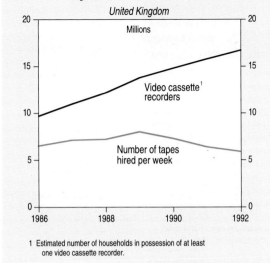

1 Estimated number of households in possession of at least one video cassette recorder.

Source: British Videogram Association

From: Social Trends 1994, Chart 10.6

12.3 Reading of national newspapers: by sex and age, 1992
Great Britain

	Percentage of adults reading each paper in 1992			Percentage of each age group reading each paper in 1992				Readership[1] (millions)		Readers per copy (numbers)
	Males	Females	All adults	15-24	25-44	45-64	65 and over	1971	1992	1992
Daily newspapers										
The Sun	24	19	21	28	23	20	15	8.5	9.7	2.7
Daily Mirror	19	15	17	18	16	18	17	13.8	7.8	2.8
Daily Mail	10	10	10	8	9	11	11	4.8	4.5	2.6
Daily Express	9	8	8	7	6	10	11	9.7	3.8	2.5
The Daily Telegraph	6	5	6	4	4	7	7	3.6	2.5	2.4
Daily Star	7	4	5	8	6	5	2	.	2.4	3.0
Today	4	3	3	4	4	3	2	.	1.5	2.9
The Guardian	3	2	3	3	4	3	1	1.1	1.3	3.1
The Independent	3	2	2	2	3	2	1	.	1.1	2.9
The Times	3	2	2	2	2	3	1	1.1	1.0	2.7
Financial Times	2	1	1	1	2	1	-	0.7	0.6	3.6
Any national daily newspaper[2]	65	56	60	59	57	64	62	..	27.3	..
Sunday newspapers										
News of the World	29	26	28	35	31	26	19	15.8	12.5	2.7
Sunday Mirror	20	18	19	22	20	20	16	13.5	8.8	3.2
The People	14	13	13	13	12	15	14	14.4	6.1	2.9
The Mail on Sunday	13	13	13	14	14	14	9	.	5.8	2.9
Sunday Express	11	11	11	10	8	13	14	10.4	4.9	2.8
The Sunday Times	9	7	8	9	9	8	4	3.7	3.5	3.0
Sunday Telegraph	4	4	4	3	4	5	5	2.1	1.8	3.2
The Observer	4	3	4	4	4	4	2	2.4	1.7	3.1
Sunday Sport	5	1	3	7	3	1	-	.	1.3	4.1
Independent on Sunday	3	2	3	4	4	2	1	.	1.3	3.2
Any Sunday newspaper[3]	71	67	69	71	68	72	66	..	31.3	..

1 Defined as the average issue readership and represents the number of people who claim to have read or looked at one or more copies of a given
  publication during a period equal to the interval at which the publication appears.
2 Includes the above newspapers plus the *Daily Record*, *Sporting Life* and *Racing Post*.
3 Includes the above newspapers plus the *Sunday Post*, *Sunday Mail* and *Scotland*.

Source: National Readership Surveys Ltd
From: Social Trends 1994, Table 10.10

12.4 Television viewing: by social class

	United Kingdom	Hours and minutes and percentages	
	1986	1991	1992
Social class[1]			
(hours:mins per week)			
AB	19:50	18:51	19:56
C1	23:05	23:56	25:08
C2	26:00	26:57	27:30
DE	33:35	31:56	31:54
All persons	26:32	26:04	26:44
Reach[2]			
(percentages)			
Daily	78	79	82
Weekly	94	94	95

1 See Appendix, part 5: Social class.
2 Percentage of the United Kingdom population aged 4 and over
  who viewed TV for at least three consecutive minutes.

Sources: Broadcasters' Audience Research
Board; British Broadcasting Corporation;
AGB Limited; RSMB Limited

From: Social Trends 1994, Table 10.4

Key Data 94, © Crown copyright 1994

12.5 Participation in home-based leisure activities, 1990

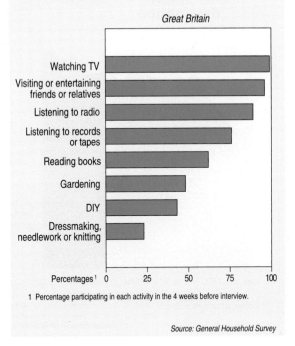

Great Britain

Watching TV
Visiting or entertaining friends or relatives
Listening to radio
Listening to records or tapes
Reading books
Gardening
DIY
Dressmaking, needlework or knitting

Percentages[1]   0   25   50   75   100

1 Percentage participating in each activity in the 4 weeks before interview.

Source: General Household Survey

From: Social Trends 1994, Chart 10.3

12.6 Trade deliveries of LPs, cassettes, compact discs and singles

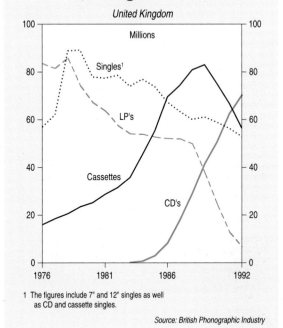

United Kingdom

Millions

Singles[1]

LP's

Cassettes

CD's

1976   1981   1986   1992

1 The figures include 7" and 12" singles as well as CD and cassette singles.

Source: British Phonographic Industry

From: Social Trends 1994, Chart 10.8

12.7 Participation in the most popular sports, games and physical activities: by age, 1990

Great Britain   Percentages and numbers

	16-19	20-24	25-29	30-44	45-59	60-69	70 and over	All aged 16 and over	Median age of partic- ipants
Percentage in each group participating in each activity in the 12 months before interview									
Walking	72	70	73	73	69	61	37	65	41
Swimming	70	65	63	58	35	20	6	42	34
Snooker, pool, billiards	56	46	37	25	13	7	3	22	29
Keep fit, yoga	31	35	31	23	14	9	5	19	33
Cycling	41	23	22	22	13	8	4	17	35
Darts	29	26	21	15	10	4	2	13	31
Golf	21	19	18	15	11	7	2	12	35
Tenpin bowls, skittles	26	26	19	15	7	2	1	11	30
Running, jogging	30	20	18	13	3	1	-	9	28
Soccer	33	23	18	9	2	-	-	9	25
Weightlifting, training	27	24	20	10	3	-	-	9	27
Badminton	32	18	13	10	4	1	-	9	27
Tennis	29	16	11	9	3	1	-	7	27
Squash	15	15	15	8	2	-	-	6	27
Fishing	11	7	8	8	6	3	1	6	36

Source: General Household Survey

From: Social Trends 1994, Table 10.21

LEISURE & TOURISM

12.8 Membership of selected organisations for young people

United Kingdom   Thousands

	1971	1981	1992
Membership			
Cub Scouts[1]	265	309	349
Brownie Guides[2,3]	376	427	385
Scouts[4]	215	234	192
Girl Guides[3,5]	316	348	225
Sea Cadet Corps	18	19	18
Army Cadet Force	39	46	39
Air Training Corps	33	35	35
Combined Cadet Force	45	44	40
Boys' Brigade	140	154	100
Girls' Brigade	97	94	73
Methodist Association of Youth Clubs	115	127	60
NABC - Clubs for Young People	164	186	155
Youth Clubs UK - Boys	179	430	397
- Girls	140	341	318
National Federation of Young Farmers' Clubs[6]			
- Males	24	28	16
- Females	16	23	14
Young Men's Christian Association[7]			
- Males	35	36	46
- Females	13	19	34
Rotaract Clubs	1	10	10

1 Includes Beaver Scouts (6-8 years).
2 Includes Rainbow Guides (4 or 5-7 years).
3 Includes Guides in the Channel Islands, Isle of Man and British Guides in foreign countries.
4 Includes Venture Scouts (15$^{1/2}$ - 20 years).
5 Includes Ranger Guides (14-18 years) and young leaders (15-18 years).
6 Figures relate to England, Wales and the Channel Islands and to young people aged between 10 and 25 in 1971 and 10 and 26 in 1981 and 1992.
7 Figures relate to registered members aged under 25.

Sources: Organisations concerned
From: Social Trends 1994, Table 11.5

12.9 Holidays[1] taken by Great Britain residents: by destination

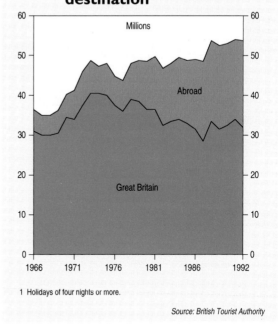

1 Holidays of four nights or more.

Source: British Tourist Authority

From: Social Trends 1994, Chart 10.26

12.10 Overseas travel and tourism: earnings and expenditure

£ million, current prices, seasonally adjusted

	Expenditure by overseas visitors to UK	Expenditure by UK residents abroad	Net earnings in UK		Expenditure by overseas visitors to UK	Expenditure by UK residents abroad	Net earnings in UK
1983	4 003	4 090	-87	1992 Aug	640	905	-265
1984	4 614	4 663	-49	Sep	649	896	-247
1985	5 442	4 871	571	Oct	612	916	-304
1986	5 553	6 083	-530	Nov	654	978	-324
1987	6 260	7 280	-1 020	Dec	706	1 030	-324
1988	6 184	8 216	-2 032	1993 Jan[1]	672	1 030	-358
1989	6 945	9 357	-2 412	Feb[1]	863	1 054	-191
1990	7 748	9 886	-2 138	Mar[1]	756	1 003	-247
1991	7 386	9 951	-2 565	Apr[1]	744	1 077	-333
1992	7 891	11 243	-3 352	May[1]	721	1 093	-372
				Jun[1]	721	1 072	-351
1992 Q3	1 915	2 698	-783				
Q4	1 972	2 924	-952	Jul[1]	757	1 057	-300
				Aug[1]	763	1 086	-323
1993 Q1[1]	2 291	3 087	-796	Sep[1]	756	1 056	-300
Q2[1]	2 185	3 241	-1 056	Oct[1]	774	1 088	-314
Q3[1]	2 275	3 198	-923	Nov[1]	794	1 059	-265
Q4[1]	2 339	3 255	-916	Dec[1]	772	1 109	-337

1 Rounded to the nearest £5 million.

Source: Department of Employment (Employment Gazette)
From: Monthly Digest, May 1994, Table 19.2
Key Data 94, © Crown copyright 1994

12.11 Attendances at selected events

Thousands

	1981	1986	1991	1993
Wimbledon	358	400	354	393
Grand National	56	53	56	50
The Derby	50	47	26	27
Varsity Rugby Match	28	38	57	66
The Open Golf Championship	112	134	192	140
Royal Tournament	280	284	266	235
Edinburgh Military Tattoo	205	192	198	210
National Eisteddfod	..	126	164	132
Biggin Hill Air Fair	57	87	61	64
London International Boat Show	243	233	232	185
Southampton International Boat Show	..	98	110	104
London Motor Show	229	..	280	363
Ideal Home Exhibition	871	752	627	551
Crufts	74	79	77	79

Sources: Organisations concerned

From: Social Trends 1994, Table 10.16

12.12 Main purpose of leisure day visits: by time of year

Great Britain   Percentages

	Jan to March	April to June	July to Sept	Oct to Dec	Total
Visit attraction	11	31	41	18	100
Theatre, bingo, etc	30	27	21	22	100
Pub, restaurant	25	21	26	28	100
Dancing	26	21	17	36	100
Visit friends	28	26	25	22	100
Outdoor activity	18	25	41	16	100
Sport	24	30	27	20	100
Shopping	22	24	20	35	100
Exhibitions	24	32	21	24	100
All visits[1]	22	26	30	23	100

1 Includes other purposes not shown separately.

Source: Department of National Heritage

From: Social Trends 1994, Table 10.17

12.13 Attendances at the most popular tourist attractions

Great Britain   Millions

	1981	1991	1992
Attractions with free admission			
Blackpool Pleasure Beach	7.5	6.5	6.5
British Museum	2.6	5.1	6.3
National Gallery	2.7	4.3	4.3
Strathclyde Country Park	..	4.2	4.2
Palace Pier, Brighton	..	3.5	3.5
Pleasure Beach, Great Yarmouth	..	2.5	2.3
Pleasureland, Southport	..	1.8	2.0
Tate Gallery	0.9	1.8	1.6
Bragdate Park	1.2	1.3	1.3
Frontierland, Morecambe	..	1.3	1.3
Victoria and Albert Museum	1.4	1.1	1.2
Attractions charging admission			
Alton Towers	1.6	2.0	2.5
Madame Tussaud's	2.0	2.2	2.3
Tower of London	2.1	1.9	2.2
Natural History Museum[1]	3.7	1.6	1.7
St Paul's Cathedral[2]	..	1.5	1.4
Tower World, Blackpool	..	1.3	1.3
Science Museum[3]	3.8	1.3	1.2
Chessington World of Adventures	0.5	1.4	1.2
Thorpe Park	0.6	0.9	1.0
Royal Academy	0.6	0.8	1.0

1 Admission charges were introduced in April 1987.
2 Admission charges were introduced in April 1991.
3 Admission charges were introduced in 1989.

Source: British Tourist Authority

From: Social Trends 1994, Table 10.18

12.14 Average attendances at football and rugby league

Great Britain				Numbers
	Football Association[1] Premier League[2]	Football League[1] Division One[3]	Scottish Football League Premier Division[4]	Rugby Football League Premier Division
1961/62	26,106	16,132	11,178	.
1966/67	30,829	15,701	8,683	.
1971/72	31,352	14,652	5,228	.
1976/77	29,540	13,529	11,844	.
1981/82	22,556	10,282	9,467	.
1986/87	19,800	9,000	11,720	4,844
1987/88	19,300	10,600	13,949	5,826
1988/89	20,600	10,600	15,708	7,292
1989/90	20,800	12,500	15,576	6,450
1990/91	22,681	11,457	14,424	6,420
1991/92	21,622	10,525	11,970	6,511
1992/93	21,125	10,641	11,520	6,170

1 League matches only until 1985/86. From 1986/87, Football League attendances include promotion and relegation play-off matches.
2 Prior to 1992/93, Football League Division One.
3 Prior to 1992/93, Football League Division Two.
4 Prior to 1976/77, Scottish League Division One.

Sources: Football Association Premier League; Football League; Scottish Football League; Rugby Football League

From: Social Trends 1994, Table 10.22

12.15 Household expenditure in real terms[1] on selected leisure items

	£ per week at 1992 prices[1] and percentages		
	1986	1991	1992
Alcoholic drink consumed away from home	8.40	7.85	7.79
Meals consumed out[2]	6.19	6.24	6.10
Books, newspapers, magazines, etc	3.86	3.80	3.84
Television, video and audio equipment			
Purchases	4.14	4.77	5.20
Rentals, including licence fees	2.81	2.31	2.39
Home computers	0.23	0.54	0.61
Purchase of materials for home repairs, etc	4.33	4.07	3.96
Holidays	7.61	10.21	11.21
Hobbies	0.09	0.13	0.07
Cinema admissions	0.14	0.19	0.19
Theatre, concert, etc admissions	0.41	0.53	0.55
Subscription and admission charges to participant sports	1.01	1.10	1.50
Spectator sports admissions	0.16	0.19	0.24
Sports goods (excluding clothes)	0.52	0.45	0.52
Other entertainment	0.70	0.84	0.88
Total weekly expenditure on above	40.61	43.24	45.04
Expenditure on above items as a percentage of total household expenditure	16.1	16.1	16.6

1 Adjusted to real terms using the Retail Prices Index.
2 Eaten on the premises, excluding state school meals and workplace meals.

From: Social Trends 1994, Table 10.29

Key Data 94, © Crown copyright 1994

Definitions and sources

Educational establishments in the United Kingdom may be administered and financed in a number of ways.

Public sector: by local education authorities, which form part of the structure of local government;

Assisted: by governing bodies which have a substantial degree of autonomy from public authorities but which receive grants direct from central government sources;

Grant maintained: since 1988 all local education authority maintained secondary, middle and primary schools can apply for Self Governing (GM) status and receive direct grants from the Department for Education. The governing body of such a school is responsible for all aspects of school management, including the deployment of funds, employment of staff and provision of most of the educational support services, staff and pupils. In January there were 75 primary and 266 secondary Self Governing (GM) schools in England and Wales;

Independent: by the private sector, including individuals, companies, and charitable institutions;

Local Management of Schools (LMS): under LMS, which was introduced in Northern Ireland in 1991, all public sector and assisted secondary schools have delegated responsibility for managing their school budgets and staff numbers, and this delegation is being extended to primary schools in these sectors.

The pupil/teacher ratios used here are the ratios of all pupils to all teachers employed on the day of annual count (with due allowance for part-timers). The count is taken in January (September in Scotland from 1974/75).

Ages are measured at 31 August for 1980/81 onwards (except in Northern Ireland; age detail has been estimated).

Further education

The term 'further education' may be used in a general sense to cover all non-advanced education after the period of compulsory education. More commonly it excludes those staying on at secondary schools, and those studying higher education at universities and other establishments. From 1993 all colleges in the Further Education Funding Councils (FEFC) Sector and further education courses in other establishments have been funded by an FEFC.

Higher education

The term 'higher education' as used here covers all advanced courses (including teacher training courses) in universities and institutions of higher and further education, that is those leading to qualifications above General Certificate of Education 'A' level, Scottish Certificate of Education 'H' grade, BTEC National Diploma and Ordinary National Diploma; or their equivalents. Since April 1993 publicly funded HE courses in the UK have been funded by the HE funding councils, the FE Funding Councils of England and Wales, the Scottish Office Education Department and the Department of Education, Northern Ireland.

There are very helpful explanatory notes given in *Social Trends* Appendix Part 3, as well as in the publications of the education departments (summarised in bulletins).

University students are counted on 31 December. All other students are counted on 1 November in England and Wales, and in October in Scotland and Northern Ireland.

Full-time includes sandwich courses; part-time includes evening only courses.

For other sources see:

Guide to Official Statistics, 1990 edition (200 pages approximately, fully indexed) HMSO.

Education Statistics for the United Kingdom, 1993 edition (102 pages approximately, fully indexed) HMSO.

13.1 School pupils[1]: by type of school[2]

United Kingdom — Thousands

	1970/71	1980/81	1990/91	1991/92
Public sector schools (full and part-time)				
Nursery	50	89	105	106
Primary	5,902	5,171	4,955	4,998
Secondary				
Under school-leaving age	..	4,202	3,044	3,083
Over school-leaving age	..	404	429	452
All secondary	3,555	4,606	3,473	3,535
Total public sector[3]	9,507	9,866	8,533	8,639
Non-maintained schools	621	619	613	614
Special schools[4] (full-time equivalent)	103	147	113	113
All schools	10,230	10,632	9,259	9,367

1 Part-time pupils are counted as one (except for special schools).
2 See Appendix, Part 3: Main categories of educational establishments and Stages of education.
3 Excludes public sector special schools.
4 Includes public and non-maintained sector.

Sources: Department for Education; The Scottish Office Education Department; Department of Education, Northern Ireland; Welsh Office

From: Social Trends 1994, Table 3.3

EDUCATION

13.2 Pupils in non-maintained schools as a percentage of all pupils[1]: by sex and age[2]

Great Britain — Percentages and thousands

	1975 /76	1980 /81	1985 /86[3]	1990 /91	1991 /92
Boys					
Under 11	4	4	5	5	5
11-15	7	6	7	8	8
16 and over	16	17	19	20	18
All boys	6	6	6	7	7
Girls					
Under 11	4	4	5	5	5
11-15	6	6	6	8	8
16 and over	13	12	14	15	15
All girls	5	5	6	7	7
All pupils (thousands)	573	568	569	619	619

1 At January.
2 Ages are as at December of the previous year for 1975/76 and 1980/81 and thereafter at previous August for England and Wales and December for Scotland.
3 Data for Scotland relate to 1984/85.

Sources: Department for Education; Welsh Office; The Scottish Office Education Department

From: Social Trends 1994, Table 3.7

13.3 Class sizes[1]: by type of school

England

	1980 /81	1985 /86	1990 /91	1991 /92
Primary schools				
Percentage of classes with:				
One teacher				
1-20 pupils	20	17	12	11
21-30 pupils	55	58	62	63
31 or more pupils	22	19	19	19
Two or more teachers	3	6	7	7
Number of classes (thousands)	161	142	147	148
Average number in class	26	26	27	27
Secondary schools				
Percentage of classes with:				
One teacher				
1-20 pupils	44	46	44	42
21-30 pupils	45	45	47	49
31 or more pupils	8	6	4	4
Two or more teachers	2	3	5	5
Number of classes (thousands)	174	155	130	131
Average number in class	22	21	21	21

1 Class size related to one selected period in each public sector school on the day of the count in January. Middle schools are included in either primary or secondary. See Appendix, Part 3: Stages of education.

Source: Department for Education

From: Social Trends 1994, Table 3.5

13.4 Pupil/teacher ratios[1]: by type of school

United Kingdom — Ratios[1]

	1970/71	1980/81	1990/91	1991/92
Public sector schools				
Nursery	26.6	21.5	21.5	21.6
Primary	27.1	22.3	21.8	21.8
Secondary[2]	17.8	16.4	15.0	15.2
All public sector schools	22.6	19.0	18.3	18.4
Non-maintained schools[3]	14.0	13.1	10.7	10.6
Special schools	10.5	7.4	5.7	5.7
All schools	22.0	18.2	17.0	17.1

1 See Appendix, Part 3: Pupil/teacher ratios.
2 Includes voluntary grammar schools in Northern Ireland from 1989/90, (formerly allocated to the non-mantained sector).
3 Excludes independent schools in Scotland in 1970/71 and in Northern Ireland in all years.

Source: Department for Education

From: Social Trends 1994, Table 3.26

Key Data 94, © Crown copyright 1994

EDUCATION

13.5 Employment in education: by type of establishment

United Kingdom			Thousands
	1970/71	1980/81	1990/91
Full-time teachers and lecturers			
Schools			
Public sector			
Primary schools[1]	203	222	210
Secondary schools[2]	199	281	234
Non-maintained schools[2,3]	36	43	45
Special schools	10	19	19
All schools	448	565	508
Establishments of further and			
higher education[4]	69	89	91
Universities[5]	29	34	32
All establishments[6]	546	693	637

1 Includes nursery schools.
2 From 1989/90 Voluntary Grammar Schools in Northern Ireland are recorded in the maintained sector.
3 Excludes independent schools in Scotland.
4 Includes former Colleges of Education.
5 Excludes The Open University and the independent University College of Buckingham.
6 Includes teachers classified as miscellaneous in England and Wales (over 6.5 thousand in 1990/91) not included elsewhere.

Source: Department for Education

From: Social Trends 1994, Table 3.25

13.6 School leavers with grades A-C at GCSE[1]: by subject and sex, 1990/91

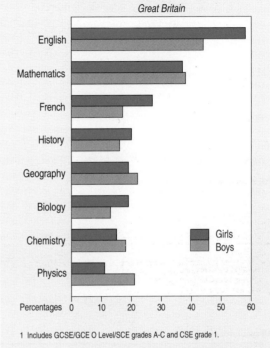

Great Britain

1 Includes GCSE/GCE O Level/SCE grades A-C and CSE grade 1.

Sources: Department for Education; Welsh Office; The Scottish Office Education Department

From: Social Trends 1994, Chart 3.20

13.7 Full and part-time students in higher education [1,2]: by sex and type of establishment

United Kingdom   Thousands

	Males					Females				
	1970 /71	1975 /76	1980 /81	1985 /86	1991 /92[3]	1970 /71	1975 /76	1980 /81	1985 /86	1991 /92[3]
Full-time and sandwich students										
Universities										
Undergraduates	134	141	157	148	178	59	77	101	108	150
Postgraduates	33	37	34	37	46	10	13	15	17	28
Other[4]										
Undergraduates	} 107	123	{ 120	146	207	} 114	123	{ 95	129	211
Postgraduates			7	7	11			6	7	12
All full-time students	274	301	318	339	442	182	214	217	261	400
Part-time students										
Universities										
Undergraduates	3	2	2	5	6	2	2	2	5	8
Postgraduates	15	17	20	22	31	3	5	8	11	23
Open University[5]	14	34	38	43	51	5	22	29	36	48
Other[4]										
Undergraduates	} 110	115	{ 138	134	144	} 12	21	{ 42	65	107
Postgraduates			9	12	21			3	5	17
All part-time students	142	168	207	215	253	23	50	86	122	202
All students	416	470	524	553	695	205	264	303	384	602

1 See Appendix, Part 3: Stages of education.
2 Excludes students enrolled on nursing and paramedic courses at Department of Health establishments.
3 Excludes 2.5 thousand non-university students in Scotland recorded as sex unknown.
4 Polytechnics and other Higher Education establishments.
5 Calendar years beginning in second year shown. Excludes short course students up to 1982/83.

Source: Department for Education
From: Social Trends 1994, Table 3.10

13.8 Full and part-time students in further education: by sex

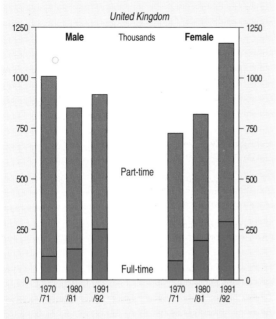

From: Social Trends 1994, Chart 3.8

Key Data 94, © Crown copyright 1994

13.9 Highest qualification held[1]: by socio-economic group of father, 1990-91

Great Britain   Percentages

	Professional	Employers and managers	Intermediate and junior non-manual	Skilled man-ual and own account non-professional	Semi-skilled manual and personal service	Unskilled manual	All Persons
Degree	32	17	17	6	4	3	10
Higher Education	19	15	18	10	7	5	11
GCE A level[2]	15	13	12	8	6	4	9
GCSE, grades A-C[2]	19	24	25	21	19	15	21
GCSE, grades D-G[2,3]	4	9	7	12	12	10	10
Foreign	4	4	4	3	2	2	3
No qualifications	7	19	18	40	50	60	35

1 Persons aged 25-59 not in full-time education. See Appendix, Part 3: Education.
2 Or equivalent.
3 Includes commercial qualifications and apprenticeships.

Source: General Household Survey
From: Social Trends 1994, Table 3.22

13.10 Student awards

England & Wales

	Standard maintenance grant[1] (£)	Real value (£) at 1992-93 prices deflated by		Average assessed contribution[2] (percentages)	Student loans[3](£)
		Retail prices index	Average earnings index		
1981/82	1,535	2,805	3,756	14	.
1982/83	1,595	2,717	3,513	19	.
1983/84	1,660	2,690	3,359	20	.
1984/85	1,775	2,747	3,385	25	.
1985/86	1,830	2,674	3,245	30	.
1986/87	1,901	2,697	3,111	30	.
1987/88	1,972	2,685	3,010	31	.
1988/89	2,050	2,636	2,876	31	.
1989/90	2,155	2,576	2,766	31	.
1990/91	2,265	2,442	2,663	24	420
1991/92	2,265	2,346	2,441	21	580
1992/93	2,265	2,265	2,265	..	715

1 Excludes those studying in London and those studying elsewhere living in the parental home. Prior to 1982/83 Oxford and Cambridge were also excluded. Since 1984/85 the grant has included an additional travel allowance of £50.
2 By parents, spouses and students as a percentage of expenditure on fees, maintenance and assessed contributions assuming full payment of parental and other contributions including a notional assessment in respect of students for whom fees only were paid by LEAs.
3 Maximum loan at current prices for students studying outside London and living away from home. Different amounts are payable in the final year.

Source: Department for Education
From: Social Trends 1994, Table 3.24

EDUCATION

13.11 Destination of first degree graduates

Great Britain		Percentages and thousands		
	Year of graduation			
	1983	1986	1988	1991
United Kingdom employment[1]	48	53	55	44
Further education on training	21	19	18	20
Believed unemployed	10	7	5	10
Overseas graduates leaving United Kingdom	4	3	4	6
Not available for employment	2	2	3	4
Overseas employment[2]	2	2	2	3
Destination not known	13	14	12	13
All first degree graduates (=100%) (thousands)	105	112	117	131

1 Permanent and temporary.
2 Home students.

Source: Department for Education

From: Social Trends 1994, Table 3.14

13.12 Expenditure per pupil[1]: by type of school, 1981-82 and 1991-92

England	Nursery and primary schools		Secondary schools	
	1981-82	1991-92	1981-82	1991-92
Expenditure on:				
Staff				
Teaching	776	986	1,091	1,501
Educational support	62	120	69	124
Premises-related	70	44	79	45
Administrative, clerical and other	11	89	14	116
Premises	60	179	71	284
Books and equipment	32	54	57	93
Other supplies[2]	4	0	19	26
Other expenditure[2]	99	46	157	76
Net unit cost[3]	1,106	1,469	1,540	2,145

1 Recurrent institutional expenditure per full-time equivalent pupil. This includes costs of providing tuition but excludes certain costs such as central administration and school meals.
2 Includes unspent balances held by schools for future use under Local Management Schemes in 1991-92.
3 The sum of expenditure on items shown in the table *less* certain charges.

Source: Department for Education

From: Social Trends 1994 Table 3.28

Key Data 94, © Crown copyright 1994

Definitions and sources

Further health statistics at regional level, including manpower, are given in *Regional Trends*.

For other sources see:
Guide to Official Statistics, 1990 edition (200 pages approximately, fully indexed) HMSO.

Health and Personal Social Services Statistics for England, HMSO

Social Security Statistics, HMSO

14.1 Expectation of life[1] at birth: by sex

United Kingdom

Year[2]

Females

Males

1 See Appendix, Part 7: Expectation of life.
2 The average number of years which a new-born baby could be expected to live if its rates of mortality at each age were those experienced in that calendar year.

Source: Government Actuary's Department

From: Social Trends 1994, Chart 7.1

14.2 National Health Service in-patient[1] summary: by ward type, 1981 and 1991-92

England   Thousands and rates

	Acute[2]	General patients elderly	Maternity	Mental illness	Mental handicap[3]	Total
1981						
Finished consultant episodes (thousands)	4,469	280	796	188	28	5,760
Average daily available beds (thousands)	145	56	18	85	47	351
In-patients episodes per available bed (rate)	31	5	44	2	1	16
1991-92						
Finished consultant episodes (thousands)	5,966	508	1,010	221	54	7,759
Average daily available beds (thousands)	115	42	14	50	21	242
In-patients episodes per available bed (rate)	52	12	72	4	3	32

1 See Appendix, Part 7: In-patient activity.
2 Wards for general patients, excluding elderly, younger physically disabled, neonate cots not in maternity units.
3 Excluding mental handicap community units.

Source: Department of Health

From: Social Trends 1994, Table 7.23

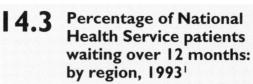

14.3 Percentage of National Health Service patients waiting over 12 months: by region, 1993[1]

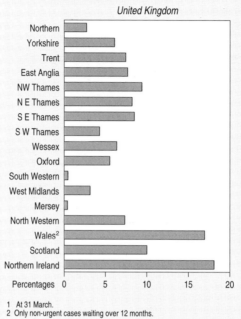

United Kingdom

Percentages 0   5   10   15   20

1 At 31 March.
2 Only non-urgent cases waiting over 12 months.

Sources: Department of Health; Welsh Office; Scottish Health Service, Common Services Agency; Department of Health and Social Services, Northern Ireland

From: Social Trends 1994, Chart 7.26

14.4 Family practitioner and dental services

United Kingdom

	General medical and pharmaceutical services						General dental services	
	Average Number of doctors[1] in practice (thousands)	Average number of patients per doctor (thousands)	Prescriptions dispensed[2] (millions)	Average total cost[3] per prescription (£)	Average number of prescriptions per person	Average prescription cost[3] per person[4] (£)	Number of dentists[5] in practice (thousands)	number of persons per dentist (thousands)
1961	23.6	2.25	233.2	0.41	4.7	1.9	11.9	4.4
1971	24.0	2.39	304.5	0.77	5.6	4.3	12.5	4.5
1981	27.5	2.15	370.0	3.46	6.6	23.0	15.2	3.7
1986	30.2	1.99	397.5	5.11	7.0	36.0	17.3	3.3
1987	30.7	1.97	413.6	5.47	7.3	40.0	17.6	3.2
1988	31.2	1.94	427.7	5.91	7.5	44.1	18.0	3.2
1989	31.5	1.91	435.8	6.26	7.5	47.2	18.4	3.1
1990	31.6	1.90	446.6	6.68	7.8	52.1	18.6	3.1
1991	31.7	1.90	467.8	7.14	8.2	58.5	18.6	3.1
1992	32.0	1.87	488.2	7.64	8.6	65.5	18.6	3.1

1 Unrestricted principals only. See Appendix, Part 7: Unrestricted principals.
2 Includes items dispensed by community pharmacists and appliance contractors only.
3 Net ingredient cost (basic cost) *less* discount, and includes dispensing fees, container allowances etc.
4 Based on the number of people on the NHS prescribing list.
5 Principals plus assistants.

Source: Department of Health
From: Social Trends 1994, Table 7.30

Key Data 94, © Crown copyright 1994

14.5 Selected causes of death[1]: by sex and age, 1992

United Kingdom

Percentages and thousands

	Under 1	1-14	15-39	40-64	65-79	80 and over	All ages
Males							
Infectious diseases	4.8	5.1	1.7	0.7	0.4	0.3	0.5
Cancer	1.0	17.3	13.5	34.3	31.6	20.9	28.0
Circulatory diseases[2]	4.0	4.0	10.7	43.8	48.2	47.3	45.5
Respiratory diseases	11.9	5.1	3.4	5.3	10.3	16.7	11.1
Injury and poisoning	17.6	34.2	52.7	6.6	1.3	1.2	4.2
All other causes	60.8	34.2	18.0	9.3	8.3	13.5	10.7
All males (=100%) (thousands)	1.1	1.3	10.2	58.4	140.9	94.9	306.6
Females							
Infectious diseases	4.3	4.8	1.9	0.6	0.4	0.3	0.4
Cancer	1.5	18.0	33.3	51.8	30.6	14.2	24.3
Circulatory diseases[2]	5.6	4.4	10.7	26.7	46.6	52.3	46.6
Respiratory diseases	10.6	5.6	3.4	5.8	9.2	13.7	11.1
Injury and poisoning	16.8	25.8	28.9	4.0	1.4	1.4	2.2
All other causes	61.3	41.4	21.8	11.1	11.8	18.0	15.3
All females (=100%) (thousands)	0.7	0.9	4.8	36.4	111.5	169.9	324.2

1 See Appendix, Part 7: Death certificates.
2 Includes heart attacks and strokes.

Sources: Office of Population Censuses and Surveys;
General Register Office (Scotland); General
Register Office (Northern Ireland)

From: Social Trends 1994, Table 7.3

14.6 AIDS: actual and projected new cases per year

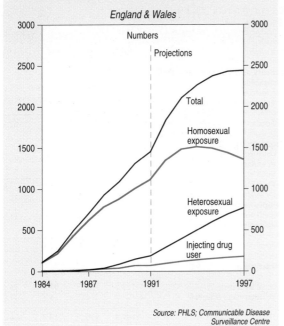

England & Wales

Source: PHLS; Communicable Disease Surveillance Centre

From: Social Trends 1994, Chart 7.8

14.7 AIDS - total cases and deaths: by exposure category, to 30 June 1993[1]

United Kingdom

Numbers

	Cases		Deaths
	Males	Females	
Sexual intercourse			
Between men	5,899		3,746
Between men and women	451	329	371
Injecting drug use	263	112	223
Blood			
Blood factor (eg haemophilia)	361	6	291
Blood/tissue transfer	13	31	27
Mother to child	43	47	43
Other/undetermined	91	14	61
Total	7,140	559	4,794

1 Cumulative reported cases and deaths up to the end June 1993.

Sources: PHLS Communicable Disease Surveillance
Centre; Communicable Diseases (Scotland) Unit

From: Social Trends 1994, Table 7.9

14.8 Consumption of alcohol above sensible limits[1]: by sex and region, 1990

Great Britain

Males — Females

	North
	Yorkshire & Humberside
	East Midlands
	East Anglia
	Greater London
	Rest of South East
	South West
	West Midlands
	North West
	Wales
	Scotland

35 30 25 20 15 10 5 0 Percentages 0 5 10 15

1 Persons aged 16 and over consuming 22 units or more for males, and 15 or more units for females, per week.

Source: General Household Survey

From: Social Trends 1994, Chart 7.18

14.9 Children in care: admissions to care and children removed to a place of safety

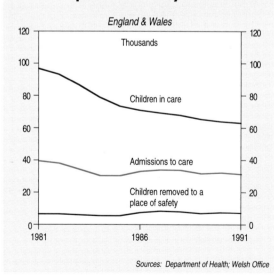

England & Wales

Thousands

Children in care

Admissions to care

Children removed to a place of safety

1981 1986 1991

Sources: Department of Health; Welsh Office

From: Social Trends 1994, Chart 7.35

14.10 Elderly and disabled residents supported by local authorities: by type of home

England   Thousands

	1982	1986	1991	1992
Elderly and younger physically disabled				
Local authority	108.7	106.2	84.1	73.0
Voluntary and private[1]	17.3	7.8	7.3	9.5
Total	126.0	114.0	91.4	82.5
Mentally ill				
Local authority	2.9	2.5	2.2	1.9
Voluntary and private[1]	2.2	1.3	1.6	1.7
Total	5.1	3.8	3.8	3.6
People with learning disabilities				
Local authority	11.5	12.3	11.6	11.5
Voluntary and private[1]	5.1	4.8	7.8	8.7
Total	16.6	17.2	19.4	20.1
All persons				
Local authority	123.1	121.1	97.9	86.4
Voluntary and private[1]	24.7	14.0	16.7	19.8
Total	147.8	135.0	114.7	106.2

1 Includes supported residents in other accommodation.

Source: Department of Health

From: Social Trends 1994, Table 7.37

Key Data 94, © Crown copyright 1994

14.11 Government expenditure on the National Health Service
Years ended 31 March

£ million

	1984 /85	1985 /86	1986 /87	1987 /88	1988 /89	1989 /90	1990 /91	1991 /92	1992 /93
Current expenditure									
Central government:									
Hospitals and Community Health									
Services[1] and Family Health									
Services[2]	14 976	15 932	17 086	18 870	21 110	22 197	25 276	29 075	32 049
Administration	473	475	553	627	682	855	979	1 119	1 249
less Payments by patients:									
Hospital services	-84	-92	-99	-106	-347	-407	-453	-510	-540
Pharmaceutical services	-149	-158	-204	-256	-202	-242	-230	-248	-265
Dental services	-197	-225	-261	-290	-282	-340	-418	-445	-483
Ophthalmic services	-52	-14	-1	-1	-	-	-	-	-
Total	-482	-489	-565	-653	-831	-989	- 1 101	-1 203	-1 288
Departmental administration	137	142	171	193	206	192	228	283	308
Other central services	218	283	324	336	326	471	535	658	711
Total current expenditure	15 322	16 343	17 569	19 373	21 493	22 726	25 917	29 932	33 029
Capital expenditure									
Central government	990	1 091	1 160	1 212	1 309	2 071	1 848	1 791	1 883
Total expenditure									
Central government	16 312	17434	18 729	20 585	22 802	24 797	27 765	31 723	34 912

1 Including the school health service.
2 General Medical Services have been included in the expenditure of the Health Authorities. Therefore, Hospitals and Community Health Services and Family Practitioner Services (now Family Health Services) are not identifiable separately.

Source: Central Statistcal Office
From: Annual Abstract of Statistics 1994, Table 3.3

Definitions and sources

The main published source of information about housing in the quarterly and annual HMSO publication *Housing and Construction Statistics,* selected information for individual local authority areas, is shown in *Local Housing Statistics.*

The main source of national trend data on the state of the environment in the UK is the annual *Digest of Environmental Protection and Water Statistics.* Definitional notes and guidance on further sources are given as footnotes to the tables.
For other sources see:

Guide to Official Statistics, 1990 edition (200 pages approximately, fully indexed) HMSO.
Census 1991: Housing Topic Report.
Housing and Construction Statistics, HMSO.
Social Trends 1994, HMSO.
Digest of Environmental Protection and Water Statistics, HMSO.

15.1 Stock of dwellings: by tenure[1]

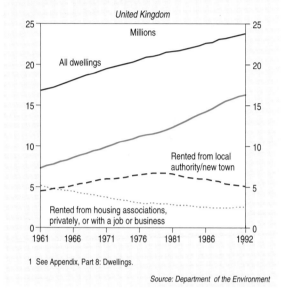

1 See Appendix, Part 8: Dwellings.

Source: Department of the Environment

From: Social Trends 1994, Chart 8.2

15.2 Building societies' mortgage interest rates

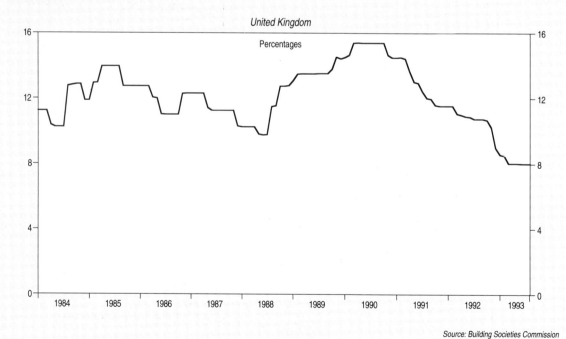

Source: Building Societies Commission

From: Social Trends 1994, Chart 8.19

15.3 Right to buy appplications for, and sales of, dwellings owned by local authorities and new towns

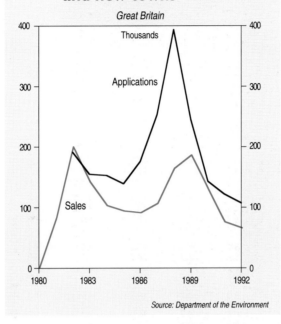

Great Britain

Source: Department of the Environment

From: Social Trends 1994, Chart 8.4

15.4 Mortgage lenders[1]: number of mortgages, arrears and possessions

United Kingdom — Thousands

| | Number of mortgages | Loans in arrears at end-period | | Properties taken into possession in period |
		By 6-12 months	By over 12 months	
1971	4,506	17.6	..	2.8
1976	5,322	16.0	..	5.0
1981	6,336	21.5	..	4.9
1986	8,138	52.1	13.0	24.1
1987	8,283	55.5	15.0	26.4
1988	8,564	42.8	10.3	18.5
1989	9,125	66.8	13.8	15.8
1990	9,415	123.1	36.1	43.9
1991	9,815	183.6	91.7	75.5
1992	9,922	205.0	147.0	68.5
1993	9,998	191.6	158.0	31.8

1 Council of Mortgage Lenders' estimates as at 31 December in each year except 1993, 30 June. Estimates only cover members of the Council, these account for 95 per cent of all mortgages outstanding.

Source: Council of Mortgage Lenders

From: Social Trends 1994, Table 8.20

15.5 Indicators of fixed investment in dwellings

	Fixed investment in dwellings (£ million, 1990 prices)	Orders received by contractors for new houses (GB) (£ million, 1990 prices)	Housing starts (GB)+			Housing completions (GB)+			Building societies		
			Private enterprise (thousands)	Housing associations (thousands)	Local authorities, new towns and government departments (thousands)	Private enterprise (thousands)	Housing associations (thousands)	Local authorities, new towns and government departments (thousands)	Commitments on new dwellings (£ million, current prices)	Advances on new dwellings (£ million, current prices)	Average price of new dwellings: mortgages approved[1,2]
1987	21 728	9 997	196.8	12.9	19.9	183.7	12.6	20.1	3 703	3 488	51 290
1988	24 809	10 260	221.4	14 5	16.4	199.5	12.8	19.7	4 832	4 696	64 615
1989	23 822	7 792	169.9	15.9	15.2	179.6	13.9	17.6	4 479	4 221	74 976
1990	20 757	5 538	135.3	18.6	8.6	159.0	16.8	16.5	3 902	3 774	78 917
1991	16 778	5 439	135.0	22.4	4.1	151.7	19.7	10.3	4 018	3 769	76 443
1992	17 395	5 400	120.2	33.8	2.7	140.0	25.7	4.6	3 386	3 355	73 093
1993	17 491	6 560	142.3	41.3	2.0	137.5	34.4	2.3	3 319	3 240	74 854
1989 Q1	6 973	..	48.3	3.9	3.6	47.0	3.6	4.5	1 030	1 030	72 262
Q2	5 784	2 021	44.9	4.2	4.3	45.9	3.1	4.3	1 163	1 084	74 799
Q3	5 673	1 719	39.4	4.1	4.0	44.0	3.8	4.2	1 150	999	75 566
Q4	5 392	1 794	37.4	3,7	3.3	42.7	3.4	4.6	1 136	1 108	76 716
1990 Q1	5 551	1 597	35.6	4.3	2.7	40.8	3.5	4.6	1 087	1 058	79 196
Q2	5 169	1 427	33.0	4.8	2.2	39.0	4.4	4.3	888	923	79 051
Q3	5 179	1 299	33.0	4.7	2.0	39.3	4.0	4.2	915	896	79 355
Q4	4 858	1 215	33.8	4.8	1.6	39.9	5.2	3.4	1 012	897	78 154
1991 Q1	4 426	1 280	31.1	5.1	1.3	35.2	4.8	3.1	927	898	76 414
Q2	4 140	1 387	34.0	5.5	1.2	38.9	5.5	3.0	1 047	938	76 640
Q3	4 128	1 409	35.4	5.7	0.9	38.6	5.1	2.3	1 037	957	76 412
Q4	4 084	1 363	34.5	6.1	0.7	39.0	4.3	1.9	1 007	976	76 056
1992 Q1	4 449	1 372	31.5	8.0	0.7	36.5	4.9	1.8	917	888	74 442
Q2	4 147	1 326	31.0	7.8	0.6	35.2	5.3	1.1	877	878	73 349
Q3	4 283	1 414	29.5	9.1	0.7	35.9	7.2	1.0	812	869	71 969
Q4	4 516	1 288	28.1	8.9	0.6	32.4	8.2	0.7	780	720	72 383
1993 Q1	4 348	1 546	34.0	12.5	0.6	34.4	8.2	0.4	829	811	74 022
Q2	4 382	1 634	35.0	10.2	0.4	34.3	8.6	0.8	840	801	75 360
Q3	4 332	1 647	35.7	9.1	0.6	33.9	8.1	0.6	796	815	75 012
Q4	4 429	1 733	37.6	9.5	0,4	34.9	9.5	0.5	854	813	74 862
1994 Q1	..	1 780	..	..	..	,.	..	..	1 039	922	..
1992 Mar		451	10.2	3.1	0.3	12.5	1.7	0.6	309	286	73 924
Apr		444	10.1	2.9	0.2	11.7	1.5	0.4	284	310	73 316
May		437	10.5	2.1	0.2	11.3	1.7	0.4	294	278	75 357
Jun		444	10.4	2.8	0.2	12.2	2.1	0.3	299	290	71 868
Jul		480	10.5	2.9	0.2	11.8	2.3	0.3	313	303	72 267
Aug		457	9 7	3.0	0.2	13.2	2.5	0.3	266	349	71 604
Sep		477	9.3	3.2	0.3	10.9	2.4	0.4	233	217	71 707
Oct		403	9.3	2.6	0.2	10.7	2.6	0.3	251	239	73 929
Nov		446	8.8	3.1	0.2	10.4	2.8	0.2	245	229	71 772
Dec		439	10.0	3.2	0.2	11.3	2.8	0.2	284	252	71 150
1993 Jan		489	10.7	4.1	0.3	10.8	2.1	0.1	266	263	73 475
Feb		525	11.3	3.8	0.2	11.6	2.6	0.1	278	265	73 752
Mar		532	12.0	4.6	0.1	12.0	3.5	0.2	285	283	74 101
Apr		573	11.6	3.6	0.1	11.7	3.4	0.2	295	266	75 019
May		496	11.6	3.3	0.1	11.9	2.7	0.3	265	268	76 320
Jun		565	11.8	3.3	0.2	10.7	2.5	0.3	280	267	75 604
Jul		522	11.3	2.8	0.2	11.1	2.5	0.2	263	262	75 216
Aug		567	12.2	2.7	0.2	11.3	2.8	0.2	259	257	74 536
Sep		558	12.2	3.6	0.2	11.5	2.8	0.2	274	296	75 476
Oct		570	12.9	3.0	0.2	11.8	3.7	0.1	264	267	74 881
Nov		593	13.4	3 8	0.1	11.4	3.1	0.2	302	266	75 021
Dec		571	11.3	2.7	0.1	11.7	2.7	0.2	288	280	74 507
1994 Jan		643†	12.1	3.2	0.1	11.7	3.8	0.1	306	279	..
Feb		536	12.9	3.6	0.1	10.4	3.0	0.4	326	293	..
Mar		602	..	..	..	..	..	..	407	350	..

1 Mortgages with building societies by private owners. The series covers only dwellings on which building societies have approved mortgages during the period. The cost of land is included.

2 The Abbey National ceased to operate as a building society in July 1989, but to ensure continuity in the data its results are included in the building society sector.

Sources: Central Statistical Office;
Department of the Environment;
Scottish Development Department;
Building Societies Association
From: Economic Trends, May 1994, Table 5.5

Key Data 94, © Crown copyright 1994

15.6 Carbon dioxide[1] emissions: by source

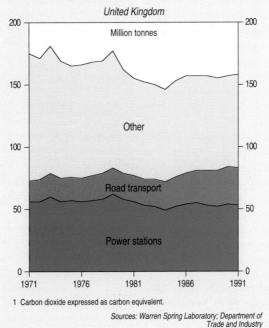

United Kingdom

Million tonnes

Other

Road transport

Power stations

1 Carbon dioxide expressed as carbon equivalent.

Sources: Warren Spring Laboratory; Department of Trade and Industry

From: Social Trends 1994, Chart 9.4

15.7 Acid rain, 1991

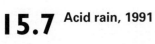

Acid in rain

Acid reaching the ground in rain

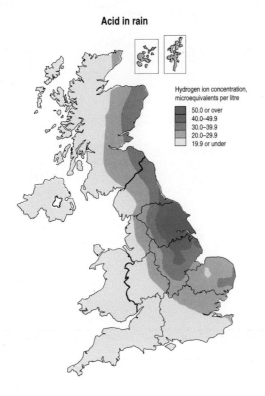

Hydrogen ion concentration, microequivalents per litre

50.0 or over
40.0–49.9
30.0–39.9
20.0–29.9
19.9 or under

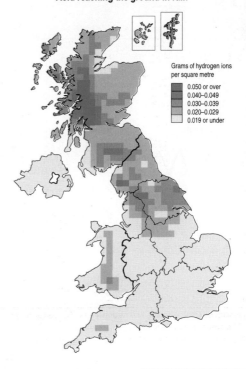

Grams of hydrogen ions per square metre

0.050 or over
0.040–0.049
0.030–0.039
0.020–0.029
0.019 or under

Source: Warren Spring Laboratory, Department of Trade and Industry

From: Regional Trends 28, Chart 11.8

Key Data 94, © Crown copyright 1994

HOUSING AND ENVIRONMENT

15.8 River and canal quality: by region, 1990

United Kingdom   Percentages

	Good	Fair	Poor	Bad
North West	55	26	15	4
Northumbria	86	11	3	-
Severn-Trent	52	37	10	1
Yorkshire	70	15	12	3
Anglian	57	36	8	-
Thames	61	32	7	-
Southern	69	23	7	1
Wessex	60	34	5	1
South West	51	30	17	2
Welsh[1]	84	9	6	1
Scotland	97	2	-	-
Northern Ireland[2]	82	15	3	-

1 Regional boundaries are based on river catchment areas and not County borders.
2 Data are for 1991.

Sources: National Rivers Authority; The Scottish Office;
Department of the Environment, Northern Ireland

From: Social Trends 1994, Table 9.10

15.9 Compliance with EC Bathing Water Directive[1] coliform standards: by coastal region, 1988 and 1993

United Kingdom   Numbers and percentages

	Identified bathing waters (numbers)		Percentage complying	
	1988	1993	1988	1993
United Kingdom	403	457	66	80
North West	33	33	18	39
Northumbrian	19	34	47	74
Yorkshire	22	22	95	95
Anglian	28	33	68	85
Thames	2	3	0	100
Southern	65	67	42	87
Wessex	38	42	79	83
South West	109	133	84	80
Welsh	48	51	77	82
England & Wales	364	418	66	79
Scotland	23	23	52	78
Nothern Ireland	16	16	88	94

1 See Appendix, Part 9: Quality of bathing water.

Sources: National Rivers Authority; The Scottish Office; Department of the Environment, Northern Ireland

From: Social Trends 1994, Table 9.11

15.10 New tree planting

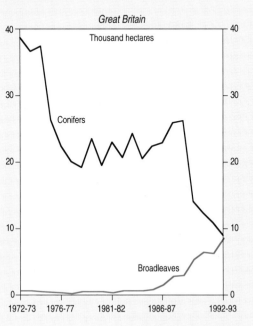

Source: Forestry Commission

From: Social Trends 1994, Chart 9.16

Key Data 94, © Crown copyright 1994

15.11 Recycled scrap as a proportion of total consumption for selected materials

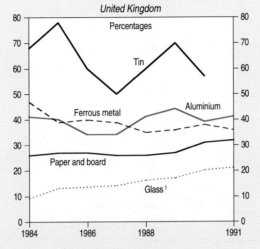

United Kingdom

Percentages

Tin

Ferrous metal

Aluminium

Paper and board

Glass[1]

1984   1986   1988   1991

1 Data not available for 1986.

Sources: Warren Spring Laboratory; Department of Trade and Industry;
Aluminium Federation and Iron and Steel Statistics Bureau;
British Paper and Board Industry Federation; British
Glass Manufacturers' Confederation

From: Social Trends 1994, Chart 9.13

Definitions and sources

All the data shown (except for the chart below) are first published in *Energy Trends* (Monthly).

Detailed definitions and sources are given in the supplementary notes to the *Monthly Digest of Statistics* and in the *Digest of United Kingdom Energy Statistics* (Annual).

For other sources see:

Guide to Official Statistics, 1990 edition (200 pages approximately, fully indexed) HMSO.

Energy Trends, DTI.

16.1 Inland energy consumption

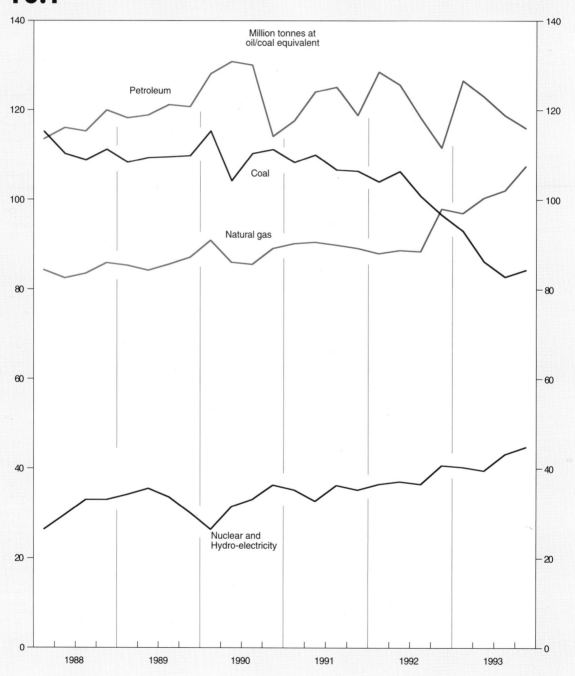

Million tonnes at oil/coal equivalent

Petroleum

Coal

Natural gas

Nuclear and Hydro-electricity

Source: Department of Trade and Industry

From: Economic Trends, May 1994, Chart 5.10

Key Data 94, © Crown copyright 1994

16.2 Inland energy consumption: primary fuel input basis

Million tonnes of oil or oil equivalent

| | Not seasonally adjusted | | | | | | | Seasonally adjusted (annual rates)[7] | | | | | | |
| | | | | Primary electricity | | | | | | | Primary electricity | | | |
	Coal[1]	Petro-leum[2]	Natural gas[3]	Nuclear	Natural flow hydro[5]	Net imports	Total	Coal[1,4]	Petro-leum[2,4]	Natural gas[3,4]	Nuclear	Natural flow hydro[5]	Net imports[6]	Total
1987	68.3	64.3	50.5	11.7	1.2	2.8	198.9	67.2	63.5	49.6	11.7	1.2	2.8	196.1
1988	65.9	68.3	47.9	13.5	1.4	3.1	200.1	65.9	68.3	49.7	13.5	1.4	3.1	201.9
1989	63.6	69.5	47.4	15.4	1.4	3.0	200.2	64.5	70.2	50.5	15.4	1.4	3.0	204.9
1990	63.8	71.3	49.0	14.2	1.6	2.9	202.7	65.0	73.3	52.4	14.2	1.6	2.9	209.3
1991	63.3	71.1	52.8	15.2	1.4	3.9	207.7	63.1	70.8	52.7	15.2	1.4	3.9	207.0
1993 Feb	4.9	5.6	6.7	1.7	0.10	0.30	19.4	53.2	68.5	59.5	17.30	1.54	4.1	204.1
Mar	5.7	6.8	6.6	1.9	0.10	0.40	21.7	54.6	70.3	53.6	19.90	1.40	4.1	204.0
Apr	3.8	5.2	4.3	1.5	0.10	0.30	15.3	51.1	71.3	56.7	20.10	1.40	4.1	204.8
May	3.8	5.1	3.5	1.3	0.10	0.30	14.0	53.3	68.6	58.2	16.00	1.40	4.1	201.6
Jun	4.1	6.6	3.2	1.7	0.10	0.30	16.0	50.2	72.8	60.0	22.30	1.40	3.4	210.3
Jul	3.4	5.3	2.5	1.3	0.10	0.30	12.8	49.2	70.2	60.4	21.00	1.50	3.6	205.9
Aug	3.4	5.2	2.7	1.3	0.10	0.30	12.9	51.7	70.1	59.1	18.40	1.50	4.0	207.3
Sep	4.2	7.0	4.0	1.8	0.10	0.40	17.5	47.5	68.3	63.3	20.80	1.40	4.1	205.5
Oct	4.0	5.5	5.1	1.5	0.10	0.30	16.6	49.5	68.9	65.0	21.20	1.37	4.2	209.6
Nov	4.6	6.0	6.6	1.4	0.06	1.30	19.0	53.4	71.8	60.7	18.50	1.30	4.2	210.9
Dec	5.0	7.2	8.4	2.1	0.15	0.30	23.2	46.5	64.2	64.9	22.10	1.27	4.1	203.0
1994 Jan	4.4	5.4	7.0	1.6	0.14	0.32	18.9	49.6	70.2	65.6	17.20	1.41	4.1	208.1
Feb	4.9	5.9	7.4	1.4	0.13	0.31	19.9	52.6	71.7	63.1	14.90	1.39	4.1	208.8

1 Consumption by fuel producers *plus* disposals (including imports) to final users *plus* (for annual unadjusted figures only) net foreign trade and stock change in other solid fuels. See also footnotes 6 and 7 to Table 16.4.
2 Inland deliveries for energy use *plus* refinery fuel and losses *minus* the differences between deliveries to and actual consumption at power stations and gasworks.
3 Including non-energy use and excluding gas flared or re-injected.
4 Also temperature corrected.
5 Excludes generation from pumped storage stations. Includes generation at wind stations.
6 Not seasonally adjusted.
7 For hydro the estimated annual out-turn.

Source: Department of Trade and Industry

From: Monthly Digest of Statistics, May 1994, Table 8.1

16.3 Coal supply and colliery manpower and productivity at BCC mines

	Thousand tonnes							BCC mines			
	Coal supply								Tonnes		
	Production						Wage earners on colliery books (thousands)	Average output[4] per manshift worked		
										Underground	
	Deep-mined	Opencast	Total[1]	Net imports	Imports[2]	Exports[3]		Overall	Total	Productions
1989	79 628	19 442	100 605	10 088	12 137	2 049	66	4.33	5.21	20.41
1990	72 899	18 880	93 508	12 250	14 783	2 533	59	4.53	5.40	21.86
1991	73 357	19 356	94 921	17 938	19 611	1 672	49	5.11	6.08	24.66
1992	65 800	18 567	84 874	19 671	20 339	668	35	6.01	7.04	28.90
1993	50 457	17 149	68 342	17 709	18 400	691	15	8.03	9.34	40.42
1993 Feb	5 166	1 517	6 713	1 348	1 400	52	33	7.2	8.5	36.7
Mar*	6 469	2 012	8 519	1 233	1 300	67	32	7.5	8.8	38.2
Apr	3 853	1 149	5 049	1 347	1 400	53	30	7.1	8.3	35.6
May	3 670	1 310	5 028	1 321	1 350	29	25	7.5	8.8	38.7
Jun*	4 329	1 620	5 975	1 358	1 400	42	21	8.0	9.3	41.0
Jul	3 822	1 270	5 132	1 515	1 550	35	21	8.9	10.2	43.5
Aug	3 168	1 167	4 435	1 456	1 500	44	20	8.5	9 9	44.0
Sep	4 537	1 662	6 244	1 801	1 850	49	20	9.1	10 5	44.1
Oct	3 859	1 367	5 382	1 408	1 500	92	19	9.2	10.6	45.2
Nov	3 689	1 416	5 212	1 371	1 450	79	18	8.8	10.1	44.9
Dec[6]	4 014	1 650	5 739	1 622	1 750	128	15	9.5	10.8	46.9
1994 Jan	2 419	783	3 227	1 578	1 650	72	14	9.5	10.9	48.5
Feb	3 116	1 301	4 442	1 355	1 500	145	13	10.3	11.8	51.6

1 Including an estimate for slurry, etc, recovered and disposed of otherwise than by the British Coal Corporation (BCC).
2 As recorded in the *Overseas Trade Statistics of the United Kingdom*.
3 Shipments as recorded by BCC; the figures may differ from those published in OTS.
4 Saleable deep-mined revenue coal.
5 Output from production faces divided by production manshifts.
6 Provisional.

Source: Department of Trade and Industry

From: Monthly Digest of Statistics, May 1994, Table 8.3

16.4 Inland use and stocks of coal

Stocks at end of period[1]

Thousand tonnes

		Inland use								
	Fuel producers (consumption)				Final users[6]					
		Secondary				Domestic				
	Primary: collieries	Power stations[2]	Coke ovens	Other conversion industries[3]	Industry[4]	House coal[4,5]	Other[7]	Miscell-aneous[8]	Total inland consumption	Stocks[9]
1989	146	82 586	10 792	1 717	6 230	3 756	1 292	1 062	107 581	39 244
1990	117	84 547	10 852	1 544	5 750	3 047	1 192	1 208	108 256	37 760
1991	112	84 017	10 011	1 501	5 951	3 150	1 628	1 144	107 513	43 321
1992	79	79 009	9 031	1 319	6 080	2 853	1 303'	945	100 620	47 207
1993	48	66 453	8 479	1 329	3 959	2 368	1 945	858	85 438	45 341
1993 Feb	6	6 327	653	105	330	198	154	100	7 873	46 767
Mar*	7	7 474	814	121	361	242	176	115	9 309	46 969
Apr	4	4 815	651	97	344	141	66	74	6 191	46 874
May	4	4 793	660	94	311	204	178	52	6 296	46 807
Jun*	4	5 080	806	118	352	229	142	44	6 775	47 170
Jul	3	4 157	656	94	272	182	120	33	5 516	47 990
Aug	1	4 208	654	100	230	185	181	33	5 592	48 409
Sep	2	5 579	817	125	294	209	188	53	7 268	49 067
Oct	4	5 284	656	106	357	164	143	65	6 777	48 808
Nov	4	5 903	668	118	411	183	177	77	7 541	47 530
Dec	5	6 360	800	139	476	241	210	116	8 345	45 341
1994 Jan	3	5 690	657	128	496	214	223	71	7 482	43 288
Feb	3	6 208	659	119	573	258	245	84	8 148	40 890

1 Stocks at end of period, Great Britain only.
2 Coal-fired power stations belonging to major electricity generating companies.
3 Low temperature carbonisation and patent fuel plants.
4 Includes estimated proportion of total imports.
5 Including miners' coal.
6 Disposals by collieries and opencast sites.
7 Anthracite, dry steam coal and imported naturally smokeless fuels.
8 Includes public administration and commerce.
9 Excluding distributed stocks held in merchants' yards, etc, mainly for the domestic market and stocks held by the industrial sector.

Source: Department of Trade and Industry
From: Monthly Digest of Statistics, May 1994, Table 8.4

16.5 Natural gas production and supply

Million therms

	GWh				Percentage of gas available for consumption in the UK		Gas transmitted: GWh[3]
	Gross gas production[1]	Exports	Imports	Gas available[2]	Indigenous	Imported	
1989	477 554	..	113 770	553 616	79.4	20.6	549 450
1990	527 583	..	79 833	569 235	86.0	14.0	568 037
1991	587 825	..	72 007	623 437	88.4	11.6	616 194
1992	597 854	620	61 255	619 286	90.1	9.9	619 921
1993	703 936	6 824	48 529	703 885	93.1	6.9	702 045
1993 Feb	72 520	274	4 982	73 687	93.2	6.8	73 657
Mar	70 700	465	4 686	71 347	93.4	6.6	72 941
Apr	54 984	452	4 586	55 856	91.8	8.2	56 066
May	43 586	465	5 075	44 953	88.7	11.3	44 391
Jun	35 990	451	1 056	33 848	96.9	3.1	31 976
Jul	33 420	697	3 470	32 963	89.5	10.5	31 173
Aug	34 393	696	2 375	33 032	92.8	7.2	32 214
Sep	41 674	294	3 666	42 028	91.3	8.7	40 790
Oct	65 165	951	4 170	64 626	93.5	6.5	63 662
Nov	83 098	902	4 194	82 450	94.9	5.1	82 511
Dec	88 441	876	4 484	87 933	94 9	5.1	89 908
1994 Jan	90 353	923	4 575	90 039	94.9	5.1	91 133
Feb	86 916	848	3 819	86 277	95.6	4.4	87 944

1 Includes waste and own use for drilling, production and pumping operations but excludes gas flared.
2 Gas available for consumption in the UK. It excludes waste, own use, gas flared and stock change. Includes net imports.
3 Gas input into inland transmission systems. It includes public gas supply, direct supply by North Sea producers, third party supplies and stock changes. Figures differ from gas available for consumption in the UK mainly because of stock changes. The figures also differ from total consumption (expressed in oil equivalent in Table 16.2) because they exclude producers' and operators' own use and losses.

Source: Department of Trade and Industry
From: Monthly Digest of Statistics, May 1994, Table 8.5

Key Data 94, © Crown copyright 1994

16.6 Fuel used by and electricity production and availability from the electricity supply industry[1]

	Million tonnes of oil or oil equivalent					Terawatt hours							
	Fuel used							Electricity supplied by type of plant					
	Coal[2]	Oil[2,3]	Nuclear electrici-ty	Hydro-electrici-ty	Total[4]	Electrici-ty generated	Own use[5]	Conven-tional steam plant[6]	Combined Cycle Gas Turbine	Nuclear	Other[7]	Total available[8]	Total electrici-ty
1989	47.39	5.52	14 24	1.22	68.38	292 90	21.19	208.68	..	59.31	3.73	271.71	290.84
1990	48.56	6.69	13.20	1.34	69.80	298.50	20.52	218.96	..	54.96	4.06	277.98	295.28
1991	48.25	5.73	14.23	1.17	69.45	301.49	20.53	218.26	0.31	59.27	3.44	280.96	302.41
1992[9]	45.29	4.88	15.91	1.40	68.61	300.36	20.92	205.90	2.96	66.27	4.31	279.44	301.40
1993	37.70	4.33	18.45	1.10	67.27	301.74	20.71	178.31	22.48	76.84	3.40	281.03	303.82
1993 Feb	3.62	0.34	1.62	0.13	5.99	26.59	1.80	16.78	0.85	6.75	0.41	24.79	26.63
Mar	4.25	0.43	1.86	0.11	7.01	31.20	2.07	19.49	1.52	7.77	0.36	29.13	31.34
Apr	2.74	0.26	1.42	0.14	4.96	21.96	1.49	12.61	1.50	5.90	0.45	20.46	22.23
May	2.73	0.29	1.21	0.06	4.69	20.86	1.50	14.18	1.28	5.02	0.16	19.36	21.12
Jun	2.88	0.39	1.65	0.06	5.52	24.91	1.85	16.01	2.18	6.89	0.16	23.06	25.01
Jul	2.32	0.29	1.28	0.05	4.40	19.47	1.37	11.02	1.59	5 35	0.14	18.10	19.69
Aug	2.36	0.26	1.24	0.06	4.38	19.50	1.35	11.18	1.60	5.18	0.19	18.15	19.87
Sep	3.13	0.38	1.74	0.05	5.90	26.52	1.88	14.89	2.38	7.23	0.14	24.64	26.88
Oct	3.00	0.35	1.40	0.07	5.40	24 27	1.66	14.28	2.26	5.85	0.22	22.61	24.41
Nov	3.37	0.42	1.36	0.05	5.91	26.73	1.77	16.20	2.97	5.64	0.15	24.96	26.76
Dec	3.61	0.51	2.10	0.13	7.13	32.54	2.16	17.62	3.56	8.76	0.44	30.39	32.66
1994 Jan	3.26	0.42	1.54	0.12	6.02	27.31	1.75	15.63	3.10	6.42	0.41	25.56	27.41
Feb	3.56	0.47	1.31	0.11	6.13	27.63	1.75	17.12	2.93	5.47	0.36	25.88	27.70

1 Fuel used and electricity generated by major power producers (National Power, PowerGen, Nuclear Electric, National Grid Company, Scottish Power, Hydro-Electric, Scottish Nuclear, NIGEN, Coolkeeragh Power Ltd, Ballyumford Power Ltd, Midlands Electricity, South Western Electricity, Teesside Power Ltd, Lakeland Power Ltd, Fibropower Ltd, Corby Power Ltd, Peterborough Power Ltd, Fibrogen Ltd and Regional Power Ltd, and electricity available through the grid in England and Wales and from distribution companies in Scotland and Northern Ireland.
2 Including quantities used in the production of steam for sale.
3 Including oil used in gas turbine and diesel plant and for lighting up coal-fired boilers and Orimulsion.
4 Including wind power, refuse-derived fuel, natural gas and sour gas.
5 Used in works and for pumping at pumped storage stations.
6 Coal oil (including Orimulsion) and mixed or dual-fired (including gas).
7 Including gas turbine, diesel, wind and hydro-electric plant.
8 Including net imports and purchases from outside sources mainly UKAEA and British Nuclear Fuels plc, and net of supplies direct from generators to final consumers.
9 For 1992 monthly figures do not sum to the annual total which covers a fifty-three week period.

Source: Department of Trade and Industry
From: Monthly Digest of Statistics, May 1994, Table 8.6

16.7 Deliveries of petroleum products for inland consumption

Thousand tonnes

	Butane and propane[1]	Naphtha (LDF) and Middle Distillate Feedstock[2]	Motor spirit Total	Motor spirit of which: Unleaded	Kerosene Aviation turbine fuel	Burning oil Premier	Burning oil Standard domestic	Gas/diesel oil Derv fuel	Gas/diesel oil Other	Fuel oil	Lubricating oils	Bitumen	Total[3,4]
1989	1 893	3 932	23 924	4 648	6 564	55	1 417	10 118	8 323	11 125	839	2 423	73 028
1990	1 969	3 477	24 312	8 255	6 589	41	1 526	10 652	8 046	11 997	822	2 491	73 943
1991	2 273	3 898	24 021	9 868	6 176	46	1 779	10 694	8 031	11 948	759	2 514	74 506
1992	1 890	3 965	24 044	11268	6 666	39	1 875	11 132	7 871	11 481	786	2 555	75 470
1993	1 917	3 777	23 742	12490	7 106	35	2 002	11 808	7 788	10 790	804	2 523	75 722
1993 Feb	142	279	1 828	919	453	5	202	906	730	998	65	199	6 107
Mar	156	381	2 142	1 086	495	4	222	1 082	819	895	73	273	6 819
Apr	125	225	1 999	1 032	549	3	152	924	595	790	69	197	5 870
May	103	264	1 959	1 027	660	1	107	939	540	809	63	213	5 874
Jun	118	390	2008	1 068	652	-	89	990	843	74		248	6189
Jul	180	331	2 050	1 082	712	1	95	997	529	931	71	246	6 399
Aug	184	353	1 982	1 054	718	1	128	954	581	766	63	225	6 251
Sep	182	193	1 994	1 076	659	4	169	1 030	648	921	68	215	6 384
Oct	183	292	1 999	1 079	654	3	169	1 032	671	750	65	215	6 333
Nov	208	307	2 092	1 136	544	4	211	1 164	756	990	71	207	6 883
Dec	163	364	1 897	1 042	518	4	235	915	673	1 168	59	149	6 497
1994 Jan	184	322	1 715	950	532	5	216	917	677	862	62	142	5 932[5]
Feb	197	280	1 733	966	474	4	272	970	729	838	60	167	6 016

1 Including amounts for petro-chemicals.
2 Now mainly petro-chemical feedstock. Prior to the October 1986 issue of the *Monthly Digest*, Middle Distillate Feedstock was included in the Gas/Diesel (Other) column.
3 Including other petroleum gases, aviation spirit, wide-cut gasoline, industrial and white spirits, petroleum wax, non-domestic standard burning oil and miscellaneous products, but excluding refinery fuel.
4 1992 and 1993 data have been revised to include the contribution to deliveries of additional information on arrivals of petroleum products
5 Provisional.

Source: Department of Trade and Industry

From: Monthly Digest of Statistics

Key Data 94, © Crown copyright 1994

Definitions and sources

Industry grouping: the industries named in the first column of the table represent the classes of the *Standard Industrial Classification*, as revised in 1980.

Employment: UK employment figures (except classes 21 and 23) are averages of the four end-quarter months' figures for GB (Department of Employment) and NI (Office of Manpower Economics). Figures for classes 21 and 23 are based on the Census of Employment 1987.

Index of Production: the official measure of value added by each industry, at constant 1985 prices; the figures therefore represent a measure of volume.

Exports and Imports: the series are derived from *Overseas Trade Statistics in the United Kingdom* (OTS) where every tariff code is allocated to an industry.

Import Penetration Ratio: imports as a percentage of UK demand (production *plus* imports *minus* exports).

For other sources see:

Guide to Official Statistics, 1990 edition (200 pages approximately, fully indexed) HMSO.

17.1 Indicators of UK Manufacturing Industrial Activity

SIC (80) Class		UK Employees (thousands)	GB employees (thousands)	Index of Production (1990=100)	Exports f.o.b. (£m)	Import c.i.f. (£m)
21	1988	2.0	2.8	113.9	22.8	732.6
Extraction of	1989	1.9	1.8	105.6	28.4	814.2
Metalliferous	1990	1.5	1.5	100.0	21.7	815.8
ores	1991	1.1	1.0	64.4	6.9	667.8
	1992	0.9	0.9	56.1	11.0	631.1
	1993	0.8	0.8	61.0	..	..
22	1988	138.6	139.4	101.8	4335.5	5402.6
Metal	1989	138.3	150.0	102.7	5265.9	6445.3
Manufacturing	1990	155.3	155.0	100.0	5589.6	6152.2
	1991	137.6	137.1	91.2	5306.7	5531.5
	1992	128.1	127.6	86.7	5043.0	5454.1
	1993	122.1	121.6	88.0	..	..
23	1988	29.6	27.5	108.9	1927.4	2123.6
Extraction of	1989	29.6	30.4	108.4	2042.2	2090.3
minerals n.e.s.	1990	33.3	31.4	100.0	1945.5	2107.1
	1991	28.4	26.6	96.5	1902.3	1992.9
	1992	27.4	25.8	90.4	1707.1	1900.3
	1993	26.5	24.9	92.0	..	..
24	1988	195.1	191.2	102.6	1239.5	1376.6
Non-Metallic	1989	195.3	198.3	105.2	1377.5	1585.9
mineral	1990	197.7	193.5	100.0	1511.6	1601.4
products	1991	175.4	171.3	90.5	1562.8	1455.5
	1992	161.2	157.2	86.7	1539.7	1470.1
	1993	149.8	146.0	89.8	..	..
25	1988	318.8	320.3	95.9	11329.2	9266.6
Chemicals	1989	321.8	324.5	100.7	12522.5	10475.7
	1990	321.0	318.2	100.0	13394.6	10926.3
	1991	230.8	304.5	102.5	13925.7	10943.9
	1992	304.5	301.9	104.8	15053.9	11714.2
	1993	298.9	296.0	107.7	..	..
26	1988	6.8	5.9	92.3	464.4	469.0
Man-made fibres	1989	7.1	6.2	98.2	566.2	490.7
	1990	7.6	6.5	100.0	655.9	497.4
	1991	7.1	5.9	104.7	665.8	471.9
	1992	6.8	5.5	108.6	664.0	512.9
	1993	6.6	5.4	106.5	..	..
31	1988	336.7	334.6	100.3	1574.9	1940.6
Metal goods	1989	335.9	331.5	102.8	1920.5	2352.6
n.e.s.	1990	314.3	312.4	100.0	2186.3	2462.0
	1991	283.8	282.2	89.4	2207.3	2386.5
	1992	265.8	264.3	86.1	2251.4	2499.6
	1993	261.9	260.3	85.0	..	..
32	1988	774.4	764.9	93.9	9225.5	8947.1
Mechanical	1989	794.0	766.6	97.8	10294.1	10282.1
Engineering	1990	747.4	739.3	100.0	11788.7	10251.0
	1991	688.7	680.8	89.8	11052.5	9293.0
	1992	640.6	632.5	85.0	11170.0	9790.0
	1993	608.6	601.2	84.0	..	..
33	1988	85.4	84.2	83.8	4961.0	5877.0
Office	1989	84.8	82.7	97.2	5753.0	7094.3
machinery &	1990	79.9	79.8	100.0	6027.6	7246.6
data processing	1991	73.2	73.0	105.6	6247.3	7122.3
equipment	1992	65.7	65.6	121.2	6302.8	7869.9
	1993	62.5	62.4	137.9	..	..
34	1988	565.3	554.9	95.3	8430.8	11049.3
Electrical &	1989	562.3	558.0	101.4	9787.5	12662.1
electronic	1990	556.3	547.8	100.0	11153.7	12744.6
machinery	1991	508.8	500.9	93.1	11479.4	12929.2
	1992	472.4	465.3	89.8	12203.1	14438.9
	1993	461.0	454.1	94.3	..	..

17.1 Indicators of UK Manufacturing Industrial Activity
continued

SIC (80) Class		UK Employees (thousands)	GB employees (thousands)	Index of Production (1990=100)	Exports f.o.b. (£m)	Import c.i.f. (£m)
35 Motor vehicles and parts	1988	269.5	268.5	99.9	5533.3	11699.2
	1989	266.3	258.6	104.9	6754.3	13485.9
	1990	249.0	246.1	100.0	8043.2	12975.6
	1991	228.0	225.2	91.4	9466.8	10651.2
	1992	223.3	220.6	92.8	9860.1	12690.2
	1993	204.3	201.7	93.3	..	..
36 Other transport equipment	1988	243.6	230.6	79.3	6042.0	4432.4
	1989	236.5	232.4	99.0	7664.3	5449.3
	1990	251.8	241.1	100.0	7572.0	6259.2
	1991	229.0	217.8	94.6	7816.0	5498.9
	1992	203.1	192.4	89.5	7317.7	5233.5
	1993	187.5	178.2	85.1	..	..
37 Instrument engineering	1988	103.8	101.1	95.2	1996.1	2300.9
	1989	101.0	96.2	95.8	2211.9	2613.6
	1990	92.9	91.9	100.0	2303.3	2684.2
	1991	90.9	89.7	96.8	2481.2	2700.0
	1992	87.2	86.0	92.0	2571.6	2837.7
	1993	83.6	82.4	94.2	..	..
41 Food, drink and tobacco	1988	575.7	544.7	98.3	4737.9	8252.3
	1989	561.8	532.3	98.7	5426.7	8999.6
	1990	548.7	529.3	100.0	5951.1	9669.6
	1991	541.0	521.6	99.6	6495.5	9720.2
	1992	520.1	500.5	101.0	7381.7	10696.2
	1993	508.3	488.7	101.1	..	..
42 Sugar and sugar by - products	1988	8.4	8.4	102.7	72.2	471.5
	1989	23.6	7.6	96.2	94.8	487.2
	1990	..	6.9	100.0	96.1	515.3
	1991	..	..	94.4	75.8	541.1
	1992	5.0	5.0	104.0	108.7	602.2
	1993	4.9	4.9	111.9	..	..
43 Textiles	1988	240.2	227.3	108.6	2131.9	4109.1
	1989	224.2	207.0	104.1	2314.4	4302.3
	1990	198.2	188.2	100.0	2483.1	4515.8
	1991	182.8	173.1	90.4	2449.5	4477.0
	1992	179.3	169.7	89.6	2627.4	4798.3
	1993	178.4	168.6	90.0	..	..
44 Leather and leather goods	1988	21.1	20.8	114.1	322.1	502.8
	1989	20.0	19.5	113.9	374.1	553.4
	1990	18.9	18.6	100.0	394.2	576.1
	1991	16.6	16.4	84.6	340.7	491.1
	1992	16.0	15.7	83.2	360.6	516.8
	1993	16.0	15.7	83.4	..	..
45 Footwear and clothing	1988	316.1	296.4	103.3	1344.7	3381.3
	1989	307.8	285.8	100.3	1383.6	3759.9
	1990	281.1	263.9	100.0	1632.4	4212.6
	1991	245.0	228.7	89.7	1799.8	4269.2
	1992	241.9	227.0	89.8	1933.9	441.7
	1993	258.9	244.4	90.9	..	..
46 Timber and wooden furniture	1988	244.6	237.3	102.1	395.0	3100.6
	1989	250.7	244.6	101.5	442.5	3247.9
	1990	242.5	237.1	100.0	519.6	3212.2
	1991	216.1	210.6	86.9	539.2	2660.6
	1992	205.2	199.8	86.0	591.5	2692.4
	1993	212.0	206.8	87.2	..	..
47 Paper, printing and publishing	1988	487.8	481.7	93.1	2096.8	5135.4
	1989	497.8	488.1	97.8	2365.2	5778.3
	1990	487.9	481.8	100.0	2846.6	5724.9
	1991	467.6	461.4	95.1	2926.8	5411.5
	1992	456.7	450.4	95.7	3094.8	5432.2
	1993	457.0	450.7	99.1	..	..
48 Rubber and plastics processing	1988	219.5	210.4	92.5	2008.8	2874.3
	1989	223.7	215.4	97.2	2266.0	3117.2
	1990	220.7	216.2	100.0	2602.8	3318.7
	1991	206.7	202.2	94.6	2698.9	3240.2
	1992	199.9	195.7	96.6	2923.8	3557.5
	1993	198.3	193.6	101.0	..	..
49 Other manufacturing industries	1988	76.2	73.0	93.3	1204.3	1917.0
	1989	79.7	77.4	98.5	1387.6	2404.8
	1990	79.1	78.6	100.0	1446.6	2401.5
	1991	70.2	69.7	87.1	1372.1	2215.2
	1992	65.8	65.4	84.4	1490.2	2420.4
	1993	62.4	62.0	80.4	..	..

Source: Industrial Economic Indicators Database (DTI)

Key Data 94, © Crown copyright 1994

INDEX

Central
Statistical
Office

ESSENTIAL READING

Social Trends is essential reading for those involved in social policy and social work both inside and outside government. It has also become an essential book for market researchers, journalists and other commentators as well as students and businessmen.

Social Trends draws together statistics from a wide range of government departments and other organisations to paint a broad picture of British society today.

13 chapters each focus on a different social policy area, described in tables, charts and explanatory text.

From HMSO and through good booksellers

Social Trends

Published for the Central Statistical Office by HMSO
£27 net
ISBN 0-11-620604-7

Central
Statistical
Office

FACTS AT YOUR FINGERTIPS

*Do you need key data on what makes Britain tick?
And need it regularly?*

If so, there's no better source than the *Monthly Digest of Statistics* from the Central Statistical Office. For £7.75
you get basic statistics on 20 subjects including

- population
- employment
- prices

- production
- output
- energy

- engineering
- construction
- transport

- catering
- national and overseas finance

Mostly monthly and quarterly estimates for at least two years. Annual figures for several more years.

A "must" for those who need to keep their fingers on the pulse of Britain.

From HMSO and through good booksellers.

Monthly Digest of Statistics

Published for the Central Statistical Office by HMSO.
Price £7.75 net
ISSN 0308 6666
(Annual subscription including postage £88 net)